LOUIS RIEL

BY DAN ASFAR & TIM CHODAN

The Publisher: Folklore Publishing

Distributed by: Lone Pine Publishing
10145–81 Avenue
Edmonton, AB T6E 1W9
Canada

Website: www.folklorepublishing.com

National Library of Canada Cataloguing in Publication Data
Asfar, Dan, 1973–

Louis Riel / Dan Asfar, Tim Chodan.
(Legends series)

Includes bibliographical references.
ISBN 1-894864-05-0

1. Riel, Louis, 1844–55. 2. Red River Rebellion, 1869–70—Biography. 3. Riel Rebellion, 1885—Biography. 4. Métis—Prairie Provinces—Biography. I. Chodan, Tim, 1970–II. Title. III. Series: Legends series (Edmonton, Alta.)

FC3217.1.R53A93 2003   971.05'1'092   C2003-910732-9
F1060.9.R53A93 2003

Project Director: Faye Boer

Photography credits: Every effort has been made to accurately credit the sources of photographs. Any errors or omissions should be directed to the publisher for changes in future editions. *Photographs courtesy of* Glenbow Archives, Calgary, Canada (p. 1, NA-2631-1; p. 22, NA-741-3; pp. 41 & 134, NA-1406-214; Cover and p. 49, NA-325-9; p. 62, NA-1375-3; p. 73, NA-2929-1; p. 103, NA-20-8; p. 123, NA-3432-2; p. 152, NA-3055-12, p. 194, NA-343-1; p. 203, NA-1315-18; p. 213, NA-1480-39); National Archives of Canada (p. 13, C-29698; p. 36, C-6513; p. 170, C-47151, p. 172, C-15468; p. 205, PA-12197; p. 222, C-1879); Archives of Manitoba (Cover, N5733; p. 19, N14625; p. 32, N10480; p. 44, N16163; p. 81, N16492; p. 116, N10161; p. 208, N9289); Saskatchewan Archives Board (p. 77, R-B714; p. 83, R-B635; p. 94, R-B 684; p. 150, R-A2305; p. 170, R-A 5680; p. 175, R-B7080; p. 183, R-A2517; p. 211, R-A7518; p. 219, R-B4524); Toronto Public Library (p. 16, T14356).

PC: P6

Contents

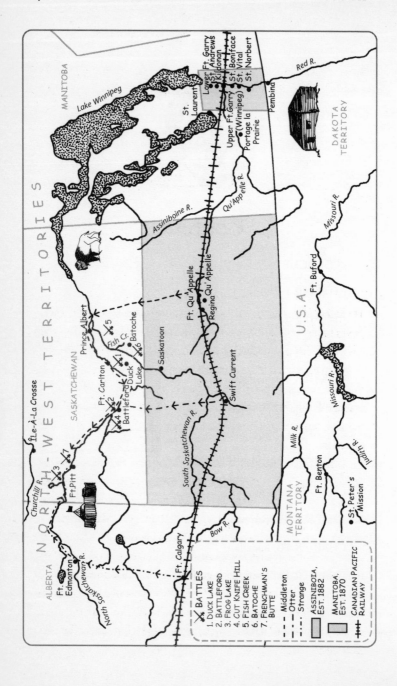

Prologue

THERE ARE FEW PEOPLE in Canadian history whose lives lend themselves to a dramatic telling as well as Louis Riel's. A man who has alternately been described as a frontier hero, a Father of Confederation, an egotistical maniac and a religious zealot, Riel left a legacy that has aroused no shortage of controversy over the years. But whether he has been lauded as a hero or vilified as a murderer, there has always been one constant in every biography of Louis Riel: injustice.

Injustice. It is the word between every line of Riel's story. He struggled against unremitting injustice throughout his entire adult life, only to be martyred by injustice in the end. The sort of wrong that plagued Louis Riel was an entity that lies beyond most readers' experience. Louis' injustice had nothing to do with the sort of personal problems so many of us struggle with. Personal relationships that leave us sour, hard work gone unnoticed, business scams or political swindles: difficulties all, but still, most of us should consider ourselves fortunate if we have never had to deal with the sort of injustice Louis Riel and the Métis contended with during Canada's early years.

The type of inequality that Riel stood against in western Canada from 1869 to 1885 was the same beast that had ravaged many other populations in other times and other places. It was the same scourge that put the Irish under the boot heel of the British Crown, condemned the Australian Aborigines to be second-class persons in their own land and saw African men and women sold into slavery for American plantations. It was the belief that led the Spanish conquistadors to assume that everything they found among the Central American natives was theirs for the taking.

To call this injustice "racism" is misleading. For while all such historical movements were indeed based on dehumanizing racial standards, they were also fuelled by established institutions that sought to exploit racist ideology for their own gain. The Spanish plundered the New World for its gold and enslaved its natives. The United States waged war on its indigenous populations to make way for the wave of homesteaders that would occupy the square grids of farmland drawn across the nation. It was an order driven by racism and the pursuit of wealth, where disenfranchised minorities or technologically inferior native peoples were subjugated by imperial centers of power. For Louis Riel, the central power was Ottawa, and the disenfranchised people were his own—the Métis.

The Métis were a French-speaking people living in western Canada who drew their ancestry from both whites and Natives. They were the offspring of French fur traders and Native women who married during traders' sojourns in Rupert's Land. These early traders (*voyageurs*) began taking Native brides as early as the 1700s, finding that marriage into a Native family cemented financial relationships between traders and tribes. In addition, their brides provided invaluable assistance with the day-to-day challenges of survival in an unfamiliar land.

Over time, the Métis (French for "half-caste") formed a distinct population. They developed buffalo-hunting practices of their own and competed against bordering Natives for hunting grounds. When the Hudson's Bay Company tried to curtail the pemmican trade that was a key part of their economy in 1814, the Métis took up arms, defeating HBC authority at the Battle of Seven Oaks. When the Hudson's Bay Company tried to restrict Métis trade with Americans just south of the border, Jean-Louis Riel (Louis Riel's father) helped to win the Métis their right to free trade in the 1849 Sayer Trail. The Métis continued to grow throughout the 19th century, their biggest settlement forming around the Red River, where they numbered nearly 10,000 souls in 1869. By then, they were also in firm possession of an identity, a common heritage and a way of life defining them as a people, and their common struggles for survival uniting them as a community.

That was also the year that the Métis were about to face their biggest challenge. For even as the hard life in the Red River was growing evermore difficult—with the thinning buffalo herds, prevailing drought and plagues of locusts—a larger, much more threatening problem loomed on the eastern horizon. The Canadian government and those teeming masses it represented were about to turn their eyes westward to the wide-open territory they assumed belonged to the Queen and her subjects, despite—or perhaps even to spite—the Métis and Natives inhabitants.

This is the story of Louis Riel's struggle against a government and a people whose racist beliefs and ambitions left the Métis no room in their own country. And while the following pages do not claim to take into account every influence, motivation and inspiration that compelled Louis Riel to do the extraordinary things that he did, it is the authors' belief that we have captured some of the spirit of the man who would become Canada's greatest naysayer.

CHAPTER ONE

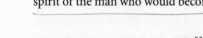

Offense

ANDRÉ NAULT WATCHED as six men in horse-drawn wagons appeared on the western horizon. The men gazed listlessly at the surrounding countryside, their heads lolling and jerking on sore necks as their wagons lurched over the rough prairie. He saw a gray-haired fellow with small shoulders and enormous muttonchop whiskers riding on the passenger side of the lead wagon. The man tapped his driver on the back and held up his open hand. The small wagon train stopped. One by one, the men jumped out of their wagons and promptly began unloading their equipment, setting up a transit on a tripod, unpacking marking poles and surveying chains. The man with the enormous sideburns called out orders, directing the land-surveying party with a distinct military bearing.

To say that André was unhappy about the sight of the men before him would have been an understatement. André was out looking over his cattle on Edouard Marion's pasture when the surveyors' wagons came into sight. He did not know who these men were, but he knew what they were doing and why they were here. André looked from where his small herd was grazing to the half-dozen men in the distance who were busy drawing their imaginary lines across

Edouard's land, carving the prairie into the square 180-acre lots decreed by the Canadian government. He could not stand idly by and watch this happen.

"*Tabernac,*" the young Métis man swore to himself and rode out to where the surveyors were working.

"You there!" he called out to the men when he was within earshot. "What do you think you're doing? This land is owned by Edouard Marion."

The puzzled surveyors looked at each other, not sure what to do. André was speaking in French, which none of them understood. The gray-haired man with the muttonchops stepped forward.

"I am Colonel John Stoughton Dennis," he said slowly and loudly in English, enunciating each syllable. "I have been charged by the Dominion government to survey this land. If you have issue with this, you can take it up with Her Majesty's representatives." The Colonel then turned to his party and nodded. "Keep at it."

André looked at the surveying crew in anger. Though he didn't understand English, he could tell that these men intended to finish what they came to do.

"I said get out of here!" the young Métis man yelled again in French. "This isn't your land! You're trespassing!"

If any of the surveyors paused at the angry young man's tirade, it was only for a moment. Colonel Dennis didn't look away from the transit when he spoke.

"Ignore him."

When it became obvious that he wasn't accomplishing anything, André spun around and set spurs to his horse, galloping as fast as his mount could take him to Marion's home. He found the Métis rancher behind his house splitting logs for the coming winter.

"Edouard!" André shouted as he reined in his horse. "There is a gang of Canadian surveyors on your hay lot. I told them the land was yours, but they wouldn't listen."

Edouard Marion looked at André. "So, they've arrived at last," he said, with more than a little resignation in his voice.

Marion turned his back on the breathless messenger and walked a few paces away. He stared thoughtfully at the dark, foreboding clouds that hung low over the sprawling prairie. A sudden gust of wind picked up, carrying with it a sharp bite from the north, a hint of the frigid season that was about to descend over the land.

"Well," Edouard said under his breath, "I guess it was only a matter of time." Letting out a long sigh, he turned back to André. "Get some men together," he said, "let's go see what we can do about these…Canadians."

Within the hour, 13 Métis horsemen were gathered around Edouard Marion and André Nault. They were fully aware of why they had been called together, and they bore the knowledge with dark scowls and fierce determination. For the most part, these Métis were physical men used to providing physical solutions to the mostly physical problems that life on the frontier presented. This was clear with one look at the riders assembled at the Marion farm. The big, burly men sat comfortably in their well-worn saddles, their hard eyes and lean faces speaking volumes of the arduous conditions under which they lived. They had long since come to accept danger and deprivation as a part of life. And so it was that they came equipped for the worst, each of the riders carrying rifles strapped onto saddles or revolvers tucked into belts. Edouard Marion surveyed the grim-looking men before him and shuddered, realizing then that this day might easily end in bloodshed.

"There isn't a man among the Canadians who speaks French," Marion said to the Métis before him. "Do any of you speak English?" He was greeted only by silence. "I do not wish to see blood spilled on my land today. It might be best if one of us could speak with them." This time a quick response came from the hulking Janvier Ritchot, one of the most respected fighters on the Red River.

"Riel," the big, bearded man said. "Let's get Louis Riel." A murmur of agreement spread through the group.

"He has just gotten back from studying in Montréal," said one. "He has spent 10 years of his life with his nose in books."

"He speaks English well," another said, "and he has no love for those Canadians who are hoping to take what is ours."

Marion nodded. "Let's ride to Riel's farm."

With these words, the band of Métis dug their heels into their horses' flanks and thundered off to find their appointed spokesman. They couldn't have known it then, but the upcoming events of that day, October 11, 1869, would mark the beginning of the Red River Resistance and thrust a young Louis Riel into the annals of Canadian history.

Louis Riel was outside his farmhouse, trying hard to contain his curses as he attempted to repair a damaged wagon. He wasn't having much luck with either the wagon or the curses. The hammer looked clumsy in his inexperienced hands, and most of his thundering blows fell wide of their intended nail heads. He had been working on the broken vehicle for most of the day when he became convinced that his unwieldy hammering was doing more harm than good.

"Oh Merciful God and His Holy Host of Saints and Angels," Louis cried into the sky after one of his errant blows landed on a thumb, "grant me the grace and patience to finish this job." If the devoutly religious man believed that all men's prayers were heard, he also doubted that God would get involved in such a trivial matter.

"Damnation," Riel muttered to himself, "I would sooner recite the Bible forwards and backwards than fix this wagon." Riel was in a dark mood. But the reasons behind his ire went far beyond his inability to repair a broken-down wagon. Indeed, Louis had been plagued by much since his return home to St. Vital on the Red River a year before on a bright summer day in 1868.

It was early in the morning of July 26 when Louis Riel was reunited with his dearly missed family, from whom he had been apart for more than 10 years. Whatever trials awaited him throughout the rest of his life, he would never forget the elation of that morning as he rode over the fields he had known as a child, watching the sun rise in a spectacular burst of color that spread across the immense western sky, lighting up his family's simple farmhouse in the fresh prairie morning. Given the kind of sentiments he was known to express regarding his family and homeland, the Métis man may well have been wiping tears of joy from his eyes as he rode towards his old home. This fierce, practically religious devotion to home and kin would be one of Riel's greatest motivators over the course of his life.

He had not left home voluntarily. Born on October 22, 1844, Louis was Jean-Louis and Julie's firstborn son and dearest child. The Riels were a close, passionate family, and they expressed intense feelings of love and devotion openly and unabashedly. Louis would always look back on his early childhood years with fondness. His robust father, Jean-Louis, was a respected member of the Red River Métis who was more than able to provide for his burgeoning family. His devout mother, Julie, was ever the doting matriarch, putting nothing but God above the well-being of her six children. So she was torn when Bishop Alexandre-Antonin Taché singled out her son for one of three scholarships to be presented to Red River boys who showed enough scholarly promise to be candidates for priesthood.

Louis stood out among his peers at an early age. A quiet, sensitive child, young Louis Riel observed the world around him with a remarkable intelligence, quick to pick up every lesson his teachers threw at him in the rough frontier school he attended. By the time Louis was a teenager, most of his classmates had quit school to tend to the necessities of survival on the Red River, taking up the rifle to hunt buffalo or the plough to till the ground. Young Louis, however, was destined for other pursuits. Fourteen years old when Bishop Taché granted him a scholarship to study at the prestigious Collège de Montréal, Louis took an eastbound wagon in June 1858 from the sparsely populated Red River to the bustling city of Montréal, where he would train to become a priest. While the Riels were loath to see their favorite son go, they were also brimming with pride at the idea of Louis becoming a man of the cloth.

Young Louis Riel, about 14 years of age, just before he began his studies at the Collège de Montréal

Riel spent the next 10 years of his life obtaining an advanced classical education at the Collège, studying the philosophy and literature of France, Rome and Greece; learning to speak Latin, Greek and English; and honing his native French tongue. His fellow students were the children of the Québec elite, yet Riel proved to be the most gifted among them, consistently placing at the top of his class year after year. That was until January 1864.

Louis was midway through his sixth year of study at the Collège when he got the news that his father had died. Riel had never forgotten about his family while he studied in Montréal, writing his mother regularly from within the cloistered walls of the Collège. Whenever the pressures of student life got to him, he would lose himself in memories of the Red River: the wide-open prairie, the enormous western sky at sunset, the unfailing kindness of his father and the peace in his mother's eyes.

He was never the same after he learned of his father's death. No longer able to concentrate on his studies, the distracted young man's marks suffered, and it wasn't long before he began looking for alternatives to the priest's life. He found his escape in a young woman named Marie Guernon, a French-Canadian belle who lived next door to Louis' uncle John Lee. The Lees were Louis' only relatives in Montréal—a contact that he put to good use the moment he first caught sight of Miss Guernon staring at him from across the street.

Whether he was enthralled by the considerable charms of Marie Guernon, in need of an excuse to get away from the clergy or driven by an urge to fill the emptiness left by his father's death, Louis fell for Marie the very moment he saw her. It wasn't long before the eloquent young man wooed her into believing that they were made for each other. By all accounts, it wasn't such a hard sell. Riel had grown to be a striking young man who bore the robust physical characteristics of his Métis bloodline with a peculiar sort of gentility. He was a rare kind of man indeed, whose demeanor pitted his frontier roots against an urban civility that years of formal education had cultivated in him. There were few who looked into Riel's dark eyes and did not wonder what sort of thoughts they concealed.

Regardless, Louis' tryst with Marie Guernon lasted just long enough to convince him that he lacked a priestly temperament. Soon after Marie's parents forbade the union because of his part-Native blood, he dropped out of the Collège, putting the world of dusty libraries and sheltered dormitories behind him forever. He quit just four months shy of receiving his baccalaureate.

Picking up odd jobs here and there, Riel sent a portion of all pay he earned back to his widowed mother on the Red River. Until, that is, the bright July morning of 1868, when he returned home, intent on helping his family survive the hard times that had fallen on all who lived in the Red River region. After 10 years he returned empty handed without a calling, a wife or a penny in his pockets, but the Riel family welcomed their errant son with open arms. The rejoicing did not last long, however, for things had changed greatly on the Red River since Louis had left home.

Poverty abounded. Grasshoppers had plagued the land over the previous few growing seasons, reducing any attempt at farming to a futile exercise. The swarms of insects covered land, houses, horses and wagons for miles around, eating everything and anything that was green and grew. The buffalo herds had been dwindling for years, but 1868 marked the first year that the celebrated Métis buffalo hunt was a complete failure. Moreover, the centuries-old fur trade of the North-West was also failing, as Europeans lost their interest in beaver felt hats that had sustained the Hudson's Bay Company for so many generations. Those Métis who relied upon the fur trade for their economic survival suddenly found themselves in dire straits. The combination of all these factors led to a terrible depression among the Métis on the Red River.

Many families were on the brink of starvation. It got so bad that the notoriously stingy Hudson's Bay Company began donating some money to the hard-pressed inhabitants. When word of the dire situation spread abroad, charitable donations began arriving from citizens of Canada, the United States and Britain. The Canadian government, too, arranged for a make-work project in Red River. Taking advantage of a largely idle Métis workforce, the government commissioned the extension of the Dawson Road from the Lake of the Woods to Red River. Yet this project was hardly charity without motive. It was well known at the time that Canada wished to acquire

A store in Fort Garry

Rupert's Land from the Hudson's Bay Company, and an improved
land route to the East certainly fit hand in glove with Ottawa's plans.
The fact that the scheme was initiated by federal Minister of Public
Works, John McDougall, who was also a staunch member of the
Orange Order and a rabid racist, hardly clarified the boundary
between philanthropy and self-interest. Was the extension of the
Dawson Road a means to alleviate Métis poverty or a way to facilitate
the immigration of English-speaking settlers to the region? Those

Red River Métis who asked themselves this question were never too comfortable with the answer. Certainly Louis Riel was not.

Riel had been back at Red River for four months when the Dawson Road construction party, headed by John Snow, arrived. At first, the Canadian road crew and the employment opportunities it provided were most welcome in the nearly starving, cash-strapped community. But it wouldn't be long before the road builders strained that welcome to the breaking point. Rumblings were soon heard from the desperate Métis working for Snow and his paymaster, Charles Mair. The Red River men complained that they were paid little more than a pittance for their backbreaking work and were charged far too much for the provisions they received in lieu of wages.

Nevertheless, in such lean times, something was better than nothing, and poor pay alone was not enough to raise local hackles. It was the high-handed impudence of the expedition's leaders that added humiliation to hunger. These men behaved with a dismissive arrogance that offended many. The Canadians assumed that their government in Ottawa had already taken over the territory and treated the Métis who lived there little better than second-class citizens. While most were aware that the Canadian government was negotiating terms with the Hudson's Bay Company regarding the acquisition of Rupert's Land, few of the 12,000 souls living on the Red River were happy that they were being excluded from these talks. Their economic independence crumbling, the lands they lived on being sold off to a government that exhibited too little concern for their interests—who could blame the Métis for feeling insecure?

The Métis perception of the Canadian government had already been colored in dubious shades by the behavior of the few Canadians who had been arriving from the East over the past years. Worst among these was one John Christian Schultz, a man who would eventually become the bitter, almost pathologically vengeful enemy of Louis Riel. Schultz was a living distillation of the colonial arrogance that so often defined relations between colonizers and indigenes in North American history. A physical giant of a man who was not above using physical violence to get his way when verbal haranguing wasn't enough, Schultz assumed entitlement of the entire Red River practically from the moment he arrived. Wedding his own self-interest as a land speculator to his religious belief that the expansion of Canada into the North-West was the will of an Anglophone God, Schultz became the embodiment of the sort of Canadian intemperance and intolerance that would tear the Red River region apart. Yet it wasn't Schultz's belligerent assumptions that made him stand out, but his ability to make them known.

In 1867, Schultz took over the region's first, and at the time, only newspaper, the *Nor'Wester*. Since its inception in 1859, the paper had been an advocate of Canadian annexation of Rupert's Land, yet when Schultz took over editorial reins, it became a bald instrument for his ideology. As proudly as a peacock strutting its feathers, the *Nor'Wester* expressed its faction's contempt for the existing order of things and its thinly veiled desire to rule the coming Canadianized roost. It harangued and vilified the Hudson's Bay Company and its governing body in the region, the Council of Assiniboia, at every opportunity. The Council of Assiniboia was far from universally beloved in the country: there had been disagreements and troubles between it and the area's largely Métis population in the past. Still, it was the accepted form of government, the established order under which the Métis had lived for decades.

Schultz had no time for the established ways and traditions of the community into which he had moved but refused to join. To Schultz, the Métis people—half-breed and half-savage—were of little significance. The future, the right future, was obvious to him, an educated, and most importantly, *white* man. In 1867, the *Nor'wester* baldly printed its opinion that Rupert's Land rightly belonged to Canada. Whether or not the Métis and Half-breeds agreed was irrelevant to the imperious, racist Canadian. Of course, the not exactly coincidental benefits that would land in Schultz's lap after a Canadian purchase—a paid office or perhaps even profits from

Walter Bown was a dentist, Orangeman and owner of Red River's only newspaper, the *Nor'Wester,* during the Métis uprising. Established in 1859, the *Nor'Wester* was the region's first newspaper. Originally it was a voice for Canadian entrepreneurs arguing for Canada's purchase of Rupert's Land, and its earliest editorials were virulent tirades against the Hudson's Bay Company. Under John Schultz's direction, it became a soapbox for Schultz's inflammatory politics that vilified the Métis and featured Orange propaganda. The Métis imprisoned Bown when he refused to print any Métis declarations in his paper during the 1869 resistance. The *Nor'Wester* was silenced as a voice of dissent on December 2, 1869, when Riel shut the paper down.

land speculation—were not difficult for the vociferating Orangeman*
to imagine.

Thus, when Paymaster Charlie Mair and the other Canadians
on Snow's crew fell into cahoots with Schultz and his party shortly
after their arrival, it cemented the less than favorable impression the
community had of Canadians. Days after arriving, Mair accepted
Schultz's invitation to stay at his home with scarcely concealed relief
at being offered such a homey respite from, to use his words, the
"racket of a motley crowd of Half-breeds."

Soon after Mair arrived, the "Canadian Poet" took up Schultz's
standard and began making trouble in the community. He wrote
a series of letters, ostensibly to his brother—spuriously claiming
after the erupting controversy that he had never intended them to be
published—which were printed by the Toronto *Globe* and the
Montréal *Gazette*. The letters were shameless works of boosterism
propaganda, where Mair described Red River in glowing terms,
making the locust-ridden expanse out to be an earthly Eden.

"The richest country in the world," he assured his audience. "The
climate is delightful. Farming here is a pleasure—there is no toil in
it, and all who do farm are comfortable," he maintained. He then
concocted a fantastical story of a conveniently unnamed farmer,
who had arrived penniless from the East a few years before having
recently sold much of his herd to the Hudson's Bay Company for
£5000—10 years' worth of a working man's wages!

He urged his readers—and we may be forgiven if, through his
use of the plural, we presume that Charlie was aiming at a larger
circle than just his brother—to come west to the Red River country. There, the soon-to-be wealthy settler would readily "find a

---

*The Loyal Orange Institution was a Protestant Irish society founded in Ulster in
1795. Initially formed to maintain Protestant control over Northern Ireland in the
face of Catholic opposition, the order eventually spread through the rest of the
United Kingdom and its colonies, providing a meeting place for Protestants in all cor-
ners of the British Empire.

Canadian friend to assist him, in Dr. Schultz and others, and he would have no difficulty in selecting a farm." Using superlatives that would have impressed snake oil salesmen, Mair invented a stretch of impossibly rich soil he dubbed "the cake," which was 700 miles long and 400 miles wide. The fact that Schultz's kindly "assistance" would, if at all possible, include the selling of land to the freshly arrived dupe for many times what Schultz had paid for it was never mentioned, of course, but the crass, carpet-bagging intentions of Mair and Schultz were obvious to any wary observer.

This was bad enough on its own, but Mair did not content himself with writing false advertisements for hopeful settlers from the East. Along his voluble, richly fictional way, he also saw fit to slander the Métis.

"The Half-breeds are the only people here who are starving," he claimed of the preceding year's near-famine. "Five thousand of them will have to be fed this winter, and it is their own fault that they won't farm," he wrote with jarring condescension. The newly arrived yet suddenly expert Mair claimed that life had previously been idyllic and soft, "but the grasshopper put a stop to that last summer, and now the Half-breeds are on their beam-ends." As for the European farmers, the "Scottish, English and French," Mair claimed, "not one of them needs relief."

Mair also insulted the Métis women in his fatuous letters to the East, accusing them, ironically, of fomenting gossip and hatred in the community.

"Many wealthy people," he wrote, "are married to Half-breed women, who, having no coat of arms but a 'totem' to look back to, make up for the deficiency by biting at the backs of their white sisters."

Mair might have been either completely oblivious to the reaction these words would provoke when the Red River Métis got wind of them or unable to care, but he would get his comeuppance soon enough.

Up until this moment, Riel had only stood by and watched as events unfolded in the Red River. He may have participated in many

Good friends Charlie Mair (*middle right*) and John Schultz (*middle left*) pose with two others. Charles Mair (1838–1927), called the "Canadian Poet," expressed himself passionately and prolifically through gaudy, romantic poems published in a series of books. One of the founders of the racist Canada First Party, Mair's enthusiasm attracted the attention of powerful men, including William McDougall who appointed Mair as his ears and eyes in Red River before he was to take office in the North-West. Under the guise of paymaster for the Dawson Road expedition, Mair befriended John Schultz and began stirring things up. He later became a storekeeper, an officer of the Governor General's Bodyguards and a celebrated writer. Later in life, he co-founded Kelowna, BC, and finally settled in Victoria.

heated discussions about current injustices around the fireplaces of friends and family; he may have made the occasional flippant remark at a Canadian walking through St. Norbert, but he did little to express his disgust at the mounting injustice of the situation. That changed when Mair's letters were printed in Ontario and Québec. Louis could sit still no longer. If he had remained quiet until then, maybe it was because some part of him was waiting for a man of greater experience or stature to step forward to defend his people. When Mair's letters were greeted by silence, Louis realized that his people did not have a voice; the young man didn't hesitate to step up and express the collective anger of the Red River Métis.

Louis fired off an impassioned and eviscerating response to Mair, which was published in Québec's *Le Nouveau Monde*. "I am a Half-breed myself, and I say that there is nothing falser than those words. I know almost all the names of those who received help this winter, and I can assure you that they were of all colors. There are some Half-breeds who do not ask for charity, as there are some English, some Germans and some Scots, who receive it every week."

And Riel was right. The minutes of the Hudson's Bay Committee, which had overseen the distribution of relief that lean summer, revealed that every ethnic group had needed a helping hand.

"It was not, of course, enough for these Gentlemen," Riel couldn't resist the ironic sarcasm, lumping the recently arrived Canadians together, "to come to mock the distress of our country by making unfortunate people driven by hunger work dirt cheap on the Dawson Road. They had also to spread falsehood among the outside world, to lead people to believe that the relief sent to R.R. was not needed." Louis concluded his letter by mocking Mair for seeing fit to appoint himself an expert on the Red River country after being in the region only one month. Riel further advised his adversary "to stick, in future, to his verses, for in that way his writings would make up in rhyme for what they lack in reason."

It was an effective counter, though Mair received a more richly deserved response from Annie Bannatyne, wife of the prominent

Métis trader Andrew G.B. Bannatyne, when she cornered and horse-whipped the frightened scribe at the Winnipeg Post Office.

"There," the angry woman said to a cowering Mair, "now write something about how the women of Red River treat those who insult them."

If Annie's assault on Mair was made into a joke by the Red River Métis, the population took more serious notice of Louis' eloquent defense of his people. Many saw the stirrings of something great in the somber-eyed young man who had returned home just in time for the coming storm. But none of them could have known how far Riel would end up going, and in the end, falling, in the struggle to give the Métis their voice. Indeed, few guessed how big the struggle itself would get—a fight that would eventually consume the lives of many and shape the history of a nation.

The mood in the Red River changed for the worse in the spring of 1869, when the Canadian government had finally secured the annexation of Rupert's Land from the Hudson's Bay Company for a sum of £300,000. What Schultz and friends had long advocated, what the Canadian government had long coveted, finally came to pass. With the help of pressure from the British Crown, the Hudson's Bay Company sold its holdings in the North-West Territories to Canada, and the Red River was suddenly wide open for colonization. The deal would be formalized later that year on December 1, 1869.

But neither the Canadian government nor the Hudson's Bay Company had seen fit to consult with the Métis about the sale, and the Métis had many questions about their fate in the new arrangement. What would happen with the Métis land? Some had registered their holdings with the Hudson's Bay Company, but many were, in legal terms at least, nothing more than squatters. The Métis also knew that their river lot properties—which consisted of long consecutive strips of land bounded by a riverfront on one side and common pasture on the other—were contrary to Ottawa's method of dividing the land into 180-acre squares. How would the government view their holdings?

And what of their aboriginal title, by right of their Native heritage, to the prairie soil? Would the government attempt to rescind these privileges? Would Ottawa even be prepared to negotiate? How were the Canadians planning to take control of the colony's administration, and what kind of administration would they be sending? Would the Métis have any say in these matters? These and other important questions hung unanswered in the minds of the Métis in the wake of the news. Given their experience with Canadian statecraft so far—where Secretary of State for the Provinces Joseph Howe gave his unofficial endorsement of none other than the bigoted John Schultz as a representative of the Canadian government—it is hardly surprising that few Métis hoped for the best.

"The people cannot tolerate the idea of having been sold," Bishop Alexandre-Antonin Taché summed up his flock's reaction to the breaking news of the deal. Riel later elaborated on the indignation in a letter sent to President Ulysses S. Grant of the U.S. in the fall of 1870. Condemning the Canadian government's affront to democratic sensibilities, he wrote of "learning through the public press, our only medium, that we had been sold by a company of adventurers residing in London, England, with our lands, rights and liberties as so much merchandise to a foreign government." The Métis had been atrociously and unforgivably ignored, and they were angry about it.

Schultz and company were arrogant, but they weren't completely blind. They quickly attempted to redirect the Métis' wakening defiance. On July 24, a notice appeared about the settlements calling for a public meeting of Métis at the Fort Garry courthouse. On the evening of the July 29, the courthouse was filled to overflowing. The meeting had been called and was chaired by a Half-breed named William Dease, who argued that the £300,000 paid by Canada ought to be distributed among the region's inhabitants instead of simply filling the Hudson's Bay Company's coffers.

It was a base appeal to the pocketbook when much more important political issues hung in the balance. Both Riel and John Bruce, another well-respected Métis, spoke out against Dease's proposal. Besides, it was obvious to all where Dease was getting his inspiration. Everyone had noticed that Dease was friendly with Schultz. Riel and others saw through his obvious attempt to focus anger away from Canada and onto the Hudson's Bay Company. In the end, all Schultz's transparent ruse managed to accomplish was to alert the Métis to the potential threat of a Canadian establishment that thought as little of their rights as it did of their intelligence.

Still, the attempt indicated the Red River Canadians' growing confidence. Intoxicated by the notions of money and power under a Canadian administration and cocky in the face of a "Half-breed" opposition they deemed inherently inferior, Schultz's men began walking through the settlements with an even more pronounced swagger to their stride. They indulged in what one later commentator described as "an orgy of land-grabbing," staking land as widely as possible in the hopes that their claims would soon be recognized by a friendly Canadian government. In June the two road construction managers, Mair and Snow, were even brazen enough to begin pacing out land for themselves in the heart of Métis country: St. Norbert, the seat and parish of the diocese's bishop. The Métis were not so shocked as to take this lying down, however, and the two Canadians soon found themselves confronted by a determined group of Métis who, in no uncertain terms, told the interlopers to move along.

Land was key, and every player in the drama knew it. For the Métis it meant not only the basis of personal income and stability but also the key to survival for their people and their culture. If they could maintain the integrity of their settlements—French-speaking, Roman Catholic islands in a sea of Anglo-Protestants, then their communities might survive the inevitable flood of settlers from the East. The Canadians, conversely, looked at the land and saw something quite different: their future as millionaires and men of power in a Protestant, English-speaking Canada. By July, the Métis were unable to ignore the dollar signs in their rivals' eyes, and they took action against the more aggressive land speculators by organizing an armed patrol of Métis horsemen to ensure that no stranger could claim title to lands in Métis parishes.

Yet incredibly, despite the formation of these groups of armed sharpshooters, in August, the Canadian government commissioned an official land-surveying crew headed by Colonel John Stoughton Dennis to begin parceling the land into 180-acre lots. Land grabs had been heretofore limited to a few ambitious Canadian settlers, but now the government itself was endorsing the new system and without so much as a word to the people who were living there.

To his credit, Colonel Dennis consulted with Hudson's Bay Company Governor William Mactavish, who bluntly told Dennis that, considering the prevailing mood at the settlement, the proposed surveys were a bad idea. Dennis wrote to Ottawa, warning of "the considerable degree of irritation amongst the native population in view of the surveys and settlements being made." But Dennis' fledgling attempts at diplomacy were quashed. "Proceed with the survey on the plan proposed," came the reply from the government. The surveyor was at least tactful enough to begin his work as far away from the already-settled areas as possible, just north of the U.S. border. But this was only a delaying tactic; it was only a matter of time before Dennis' crew would reach the French parishes. And by the time they did, the Métis were more than willing to respond in the only way Canadians seemed to understand.

Riel had been growing increasingly angry at the Canadians' behavior throughout the summer and was ready for action when Edouard Marion, André Nault and their retinue of 13 horsemen galloped onto his farm, interrupting his tribulations with the broken wagon. They told him of the land surveyors who were staking out Marion's land.

"English speakers to a man, not a single one of them speaks our language," Marion said to Riel.

"I tried to tell them that the land was Edouard's," André Nault said, "but they didn't understand me."

"So we were wondering if you'd come with us," Marion finished.
"We need a man who can talk to these Canadian thieves, and you
have seemed so…persuasive, in the past."

Louis Riel looked up at the fierce group of riders gathered before
him and felt a sudden flush of pride. For while he had always been
proud of his Métis heritage, the young man often felt out of place
among the tough fraternity of half-blood men who had made their
way on the prairie by virtue of their pragmatic ingenuity and the
strength of their limbs. These men were unlike Louis Riel, who had
spent the last decade of his life mastering the ideas and abstractions
offered by his classical education. The physical world of the Métis
was largely foreign to the bookish young man, but here the best of
them were asking for his help. It was a service that he was more than
willing to provide.

"Give me a moment, my brothers," he said with a light burning
in his eyes. "I need to saddle my horse."

Less than a half hour later, the group of riders came thundering
down on Dennis' frightened surveying outfit. Louis Riel was at their
head. Looking down at the men with barely restrained disdain, he
addressed the surveyors in perfect English.

"Which one of you is the leader of this group?"

"I am," Dennis said with a slight tremor in his voice as he stepped
forward, "Colonel John Stoughton Dennis."

"Well, Colonel," Riel responded, "I'd like to tell you that you are
currently trespassing on Monsieur Marion's land, and it would be in
your best interest to leave at once."

"This is an outrage!" Colonel Dennis began. "I am surveying this
land by the authority of the Canadian government."

The enormous Janvier Ritchot knew enough English to recognize the words "Canadian government," and dismounting, walked
over to where the surveyors were standing. Staring Dennis straight
in the face, he brought his huge foot down on the surveyor's chain.
Louis looked from Pierre to Dennis.

"As you can see, Colonel, there will be no more surveying for you today."

The surveyors did not have to wait for Colonel Dennis' order. All at once, they packed up their equipment, hopped onto their wagons and road away.

Dennis complained to Governor Mactavish almost immediately, but Riel held firm when Mactavish confronted him about the affair.

"The Canadian government has no right to make surveys on the Territory without the expressed permission of the people of the settlement," Riel deadpanned the governor.

Riel and the Métis had drawn a line on the prairie. The Red River Resistance had begun.

CHAPTER TWO

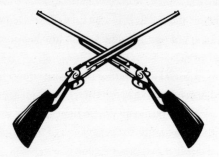

Resistance

THE WIDESPREAD DISCONTENT prevalent in the Red River region flared up into a volatile mess of conflict and acrimony after Dennis' surveying crew was tossed off Edouard Marion's land. For while life in the North-West was mostly a primitive survivalist ordeal that pitted humans against their austere environment, the communities along the Red and Assiniboine rivers proved to be as rich in division and diversity as any of Canada's teeming urban centers. The dramatic expulsion of the Canadian government's survey crew brought these differences to the fore.

The majority population around the Red River was French-speaking Métis. They were the ones most threatened by the Canadian interlopers, and thus most likely to fall in line with any sort of resistance. Yet a good number of the more established Métis, those who had been prudent enough to register their lands with the Hudson's Bay Company and thus were not in danger of losing their lands, tended to be more skittish about taking any radical stand against the Canadian establishment. If few of these Métis had any love for the Canadian newcomers, neither were they enthusiastic about backing a resistance that might be construed as treasonous to the new government. Conversely, while the English-speaking Half-breeds and old Selkirk settlers had long been at odds with the Métis and tended to side with the Hudson's Bay Company's authority, many were ambivalent about their allegiance to the Dominion government, being put off by the arrogance of the Canadian settlers and Ottawa's complete disregard for their interests.

Meanwhile, John Schultz and his faction refused to view the October 11 action as anything but treason. Aggressively and irreconcilably opposed to the Métis, Schultz's Canadians rejected any dialogue with any man, woman or child who called themselves Métis, effectively isolating themselves from the Red River community.

The region's complex political situation acquired its dissonant voice soon after October 11. Word of the Métis stand spread from household to household, and within a matter of days, the Red River was buzzing under competing currents of fear, hope, indignation, expectation, uncertainty and outrage. Heated debates over the rights of the Métis versus those of the Canadian government flared up around dinner tables, on the steps of St. Boniface Church and on the streets of Winnipeg. The region was awash in a violent flood of public opinion.

This was the political climate that existed along the Red River in October 1869, the month young Louis Riel made his incredible ascension to the leadership of a beleaguered Métis people. It cannot be said for certain what motivated Riel after October 11. Some suggest that he was driven by a fierce sense of protectiveness for the family, the people and the land he had been away from for so many years, and that he took the yoke of leadership because he knew that his background made him the one best able to bear it.

Or maybe it was a matter of principle. The Canadians' conduct on the Red River may very well have insulted the democratic sensibilities he had developed while living in Montréal. He had, after all, worked as a law clerk for the French-Canadian firebrand Rudolphe Laflamme after he dropped out of the Collège. The famous Montréal lawyer's ardent nationalist politics certainly could have rubbed off on

Dr. John Christian Schultz (1840–96), Louis' nemesis during the Red River Resistance, studied medicine at Queen's University and headed to Red River to join his brother, Henry. Discovering that little money was to be made in tending to Red River's sick, he quickly changed profession. He and his brother operated a hotel and a general store, but it was only after he linked Canadian annexation of Rupert's Land to his own personal profit potential that Schultz found his goal in life—making a fortune off land speculation and sales in his general store from a flood of Canadian settlers. He suffered defeat at the hands of Louis Riel, but eventually rose to prominence in Manitoba, where he made a tidy sum from various commercial enterprises and was appointed the province's fifth lieutenant-governor.

Louis. It is true that Louis often brought up the common past of the Red River Métis while rallying families under his cause, a tactic that Laflamme used in his search for his new Québec nationalism.

Some historians have offered another, far less flattering motive for Riel's inordinate determination, suggesting that underneath all Louis' indignation and self-sacrifice lay an ego of Napoleonic proportions, a colossal obsession with self that fueled the man's near boundless ambitions—a monolithic self-importance that dictated the direction of his politics.

Was it loyalty, duty, idealism or vanity? The truth probably lay in some combination of all these motives, each of which became more or less apparent at different times in Louis' life. Yet whatever his underlying inspirations, Riel quickly demonstrated that there could be no denying his remarkable talent for leadership. After tossing Colonel Dennis off Marion's pasture, he almost immediately began going from one Métis home to the next, describing the standoff between the Métis and the surveying crew and shoring up support for what he now saw as inevitable conflict—in one form or another—with the Canadians. While many families wouldn't have been thrilled at the news, few were left with a negative impression of the young messenger.

Louis' early rounds of the Red River were a study in democratic politicking. Greeting everyone with an easy, unaffected courtesy, he made his case passionately yet reasonably, never disregarding alternatives or opposition. Preaching about the pride of a strong "Métis nation," Riel pushed for rebellion against the encroaching Canadians. He did his best to respond to every concern and objection, and by all accounts, his best was nothing short of brilliant. Intelligent, well-informed and articulate, the charismatic Riel became the face of Métis resistance after less than a week of door-to-door campaigning, proving that while he may not have been very good with a hammer, plough or rifle, the young man understood the spirit of his people.

He also understood populist politics. Louis knew that the widespread discontent of the Red River Métis would be ineffectual if it

wasn't organized into a unified expression. Confident that he had
garnered enough support, Riel called for the parishes to meet on
October 16 in the church at St. Norbert. Many of the Métis may
have been wondering at the audacity of this strange young man,
but no one who looked Riel in the eye dared to underestimate him.
They were right not to, for as it turned out, Riel had called the
parishes together to discuss nothing less than the formation of
a governing body.

Each parish sent two representatives to the St. Norbert church on
October 16, and by the time the meeting had dispersed, the Métis
National Committee had been set up. The committee was meant to
be only a temporary organization to deal with the Canadians until
a more permanent government could be formed. The committee
was modeled on a power structure familiar to all Métis: the yearly
buffalo hunt. The hierarchy of the hunt had always functioned to
achieve a common purpose, and so it was appropriate that it be
instituted now, on the day the Métis stood against their common
adversary.

The same day the committee was formed, its representatives
voted a venerable old carpenter from St. Norbert, John Bruce, to be
their president. Louis Riel was appointed committee secretary.
Everyone present at St. Norbert, however, knew that the respected
Bruce was just a figurehead, chosen for the presidency to lend the
committee weight amongst those who hardly knew who Louis Riel
was. It was understood that the recently arrived agitator was the
real leader of the movement.

The first thing Riel did was muster an army that would actively
enforce the rule of the Métis National Committee. It was not difficult to find enough qualified men who were willing to do the job.
The prairie was full of disgruntled buffalo hunters and retired
voyageurs who had far too much free time on their hands since the
buffalo had vanished and the fur trade died off. Skilled riders and
expert marksmen, these tough Métis recruits made up a fearsome
force of over 400 strong.

It was not long before they were put to work. In October, word
of William McDougall's approach reached Red River. The Métis
knew that Prime Minister John A. Macdonald had selected
McDougall as the pending lieutenant-governor of their lands. They
weren't happy about it. McDougall was well known for his contempt for anything that was not Protestant Anglo-Saxon. A staunch
Orangeman, he had no qualms about letting his racist beliefs seep
into the function of his office. As Minister of Public Works, he was
the man ultimately responsible for the Dawson Road gang's harsh
exploitation of the Métis the previous year. Not only was
McDougall widely known to have close ties with John Schultz, but
it also came out that it was he who had made the hated Charlie
Mair paymaster of the Dawson Road project. Indeed, it would
eventually be revealed that McDougall had arranged the position of
paymaster for Mair so that the young poet could act as his eyes, ears
and hands in the territory. It speaks volumes of Macdonald's disregard for the Métis that he chose McDougall to be lieutenant-
governor of the North-West. There could hardly have been a worse
man for the job, especially given the sweeping powers McDougall
would hold.

In an act of Parliament, Macdonald's Conservatives laid out the
powers of the lieutenant-governor in the territory. They were extensive, to say the least. The governor was charged "to make, ordain and
establish all such laws, institutions and ordinances as may be necessary for peace, order and good government." The only possible
check on the lieutenant-governor's powers was a council whose
members were to be appointed by none other than himself. Four
council members had already been appointed, all Conservative
cronies who had no knowledge of or connection to the North-West.
McDougall neatly captured the spirit of things when, following his
appointment he remarked that he had just been crowned "King of
the North-West," a bad joke tinged with more than a hint of truth.
In fact, the King-in-Waiting had already arranged for a luxurious
throne-like chair to be shipped west from Toronto. When word of

John A. Macdonald (1815–91), Canada's first prime minister, had
his hands full dealing with Louis Riel and the Métis.

the chair broke in Red River, the residents were torn between fury,
befuddlement and laughter. Except, that is, for Louis Riel.

Upon hearing of McDougall's appointment to the "throne of
the North-West," he asked himself one single question: *What are
the chances that my people or any current settlers besides the Canadians
would have any say whatsoever in the incoming government?* A cur-
sory look at Ottawa's complete disregard for the Métis' interests,

coupled with the belligerent behavior of Schultz and his retinue, was all the answer Louis needed.

Riel did not hesitate in expressing his disgust to the Métis National Committee. "I hear that our appointed *King* has already selected his councillors," Louis said to the roomful of angry Métis. "Do any of you know who these men are? Are there any secret councillors among us? You, my good cousin André, have you been chosen?" Louis asked of a surprised young André Nault as the room erupted into laughter. "Or perhaps the wise McDougall is looking for a bit more experience in his officers. Father," Louis said to Father Noel-Joseph Ritchot, who stood at the back of the room, "be straight with us. Has his illustriousness asked you to join his government?"

The big, thick-bearded priest smiled and shrugged, "I am still waiting for his word, my son." The gathered Métis laughed again.

"With all due respect, Father," Riel responded, suddenly serious again, "I think your wait will be in vain. I believe that this McDougall is not interested in hearing us at all. It is all too clear to me that he and the government that sends him hold nothing but contempt for us. Not only have they foisted upon us a hateful king, but they haven't even had the good grace to tell us about it!"

The National Committee came to life with an angry buzz; a few men shouted their agreement. "Not one person has come from Ottawa to tell us of the man we are now expected to bow before; we had to read about his *coronation* in the newspaper!"

The appointment of the lieutenant-governor had been weighing heavily on the Métis since early September. Things finally came to a head on October 21, when word came that McDougall and some of his staff had arrived in the town of Pembina, just south of the American border. It did not help matters that the future lieutenant-governor was said to be carrying 350 Enfield rifles in his baggage train. Did he mean to use this armory to equip an armed militia in order to strong-arm the Métis into submission? Convinced that McDougall was not above such a tactic, the National Committee was prompted to act. The committee stationed an armed patrol on the one road that ran between Pembina and Fort Garry; they searched every traveler on the road at a barricade set up just in front of St. Norbert. As for McDougall, Riel sent two emissaries, André Nault and Janvier Ritchot (the same behemoth who had put his foot down on Colonel Dennis' surveying chain), to greet the hopeful governor at the border with orders not to let him into the North-West.

The committee's dramatic reaction to McDougall's approach swept through the Red River community. Not all Métis approved of such brazen measures. After Mass on Sunday, October 24, an argument erupted on the steps of St. Norbert's church, where several of the more conservative Métis condemned the National Committee for having gone too far. Riel's supporters shouted inflammatory responses, and the dispute quickly reached a dangerous pitch. Things got so heated that Father Ritchot, St. Norbert's presiding priest, actually feared it might come to blows. It was then that the husky priest decided it was time the church got involved.

"My children, my children!" the revered pastor yelled over the tumult, his booming voice quickly silencing the crowd. "Why do we argue so, when in essence, we all agree? We all agree that the government in Canada has treated us with slight regard. Further, we all agree that something must be done to protest such disrespect. The only matter of contention is how, exactly, we should make such a protest. Surely, we can resolve this without too much strife."

The apt summary by the respected and usually understated Ritchot doused tempers substantially; few among the devout Métis would dare to raise their voices against the Church. That evening Ritchot went even further for Riel and his committee, making the rounds of the more conservative in his flock.

"Remain neutral," he persuaded them. "You need not be party to actions you deem too radical, but do not impede them. Give Riel and his committee some leeway. See what they will accomplish." It was a watershed moment for Riel's movement because, as soon as the resistance received the Church's sanction, it was instantly lent a legitimacy, a gravity, that no amount of political wrangling could provide.

Riel stood his ground against dissenters among his own people for what he judged to be right, and he was not about to do any less with the standing authorities in the region. On October 25, he and John Bruce were summoned to appear before the moribund Council of Assiniboia. Every English-speaking member of the council was there to confront Riel, but not a single French-speaking member, except for the turncoat William Dease, was there to take his seat. Governor William Mactavish was too ill to preside over the meeting, and Judge John Black chaired in his place. It was no secret that Black had little sympathy for the Métis, and he seemed intent on chastising Riel into some sort of apology and retraction.

"Surely," he chided, "these reports that the Métis are planning to prevent McDougall from entering the Red River settlements are nothing more than unfounded rumor." It was obvious by Judge Black's smug tone that he wasn't expecting the response that he got.

"The Métis," Riel bluntly informed the council, "are determined to prevent Mr. McDougall from coming into the settlement at all hazards." The judge's sharp intake of breath was audible as Riel continued. "My people object to any government from Canada before being consulted in the matter. We are resolved to turn back any governor, no matter who appoints him, unless delegates are previously sent with whom we might negotiate the terms and conditions of any such rule."

Riel's speech may have been a little bit stilted, but the strength of the young man's composure in this roomful of adversaries was impressive. The entire council listened in disbelief as he continued.

"We are not fools, Your Honor. If a large immigration were to take place, we will most likely be crowded out of our own country. How can you think that we wouldn't act to preserve ourselves? We expect and demand to be able to negotiate terms by which Red River might enter Canada."

Somewhere, the proverbial pin dropped in the council room. Riel continued. "In so doing, we are acting not only for our own benefit, but for the benefit of the entire settlement. And we do not expect contention from our English-speaking countrymen. In fact, we fully expect them to come to our aid in securing our rights, for they have as much at stake here as we do."

Riel had been completely transparent with the shocked council. They responded with subterfuge. The council turned to Schultz's crony, William Dease, asking him to get together as many dissenting French Métis as he could and peacefully "procure" the breakup of the party that intended to keep the governor from the area. The well-funded Dease tried to bribe some of the less-reputable elements in the Métis community with money and gifts, hoping to establish a Métis force to intimidate Riel.

At the next Métis meeting held at St. Norbert on October 27, however, it became clear that Riel still enjoyed far greater support than his hastily erected opponent.

"Mr. Dease's mission has entirely failed in producing the desired result," lamented Judge Black.

It was now obvious to all that there was an uninvited but serious new player on the board. The racist belief that the Métis would be ignored, hoodwinked, divided, bought off or intimidated had been shattered. And if any vestige of such an idea remained, the Métis would soon make an even bolder statement to show how determined they were.

Janvier Richtot and André Nault arrived in the town of Pembina on October 30 carrying with them the National Committee's communiqué for William McDougall. He was an easy man to spot in the rough little town of Pembina. Dressed extravagantly in a spotless great coat, well-buffed boots and a towering silk top hat, McDougall's disdain for his frontier surroundings was obvious by the sneer that seemed to be perpetually twisted across his face.

"There," the laconic Ritchot said to his companion, pointing at the well-dressed politician, "something tells me that he's our man."

William McDougall (1822–1905), erstwhile lieutenant-governor of
the North-West, was publicly humiliated by the Red River Métis.

The pair approached McDougall on the street. "Monsieur
McDougall?" Ritchot called.

McDougall spun to face Nault and Richtot, the scowl on his face
growing to exaggerated proportions when he saw that he was being
addressed by two Métis. Ritchot spoke his carefully prepared statement slowly in his heavily accented English.

"We 'ave been sent by the National Committee of Red River to
give you this letter."

The hulking man handed McDougall a single sheet of paper. Dated October 21, 1869, it read:

Sir,

    The National Committee of the Métis Red River orders William McDougall not to enter the Territory of the North-West without special permission of the above-mentioned committee.
Louis Riel,
Secretary

McDougall looked at the words before him for long moments, unwilling, or perhaps unable, to understand what was being said. He finally looked up at the two bearded faces staring at him stoically.

"Savages," he muttered to himself as his face turned a dangerous shade of red. "You bloody savages," he said again, this time louder, addressing André and Pierre directly. "What sort of malarkey is this? 'National Committee?' Where would such a committee get its authority?" He glanced again at the sheet of paper in his hand. "And who is this Louis Riel? By God, I'll see that he's hanged from the neck for sedition." McDougall was ranting now. "Can't you damned savages see that I'm here to help you—to lift you and your people out of the muck of barbarism? I bring civilization! I bring law and order!"

Ritchot let the silence hang in the air for a moment or two, only responding when he was sure that McDougall was finished. "Whatever you say, Monsieur McDougall. But you're not to leave Pembina."

Realizing that any debate was futile, McDougall stormed away from Nault and Ritchot to his baggage train. "Provencher!" he yelled for his secretary, who promptly leapt out of one of the buggies.

"Yes, sir."

"I want you to ride ahead to Red River and talk to this…Louis Riel. Explain to him that I have been appointed lieutenant-governor of the North-West, and that he is expressly breaking the law by barring my passage."

"Yes, sir," Provencher snapped back, bowing curtly.

The next day Provencher rode ahead to seek an audience with Riel. Announcing his station and his intentions to the first Métis patrol he ran into, Provencher was promptly escorted to Father Ritchot's humble St. Norbert home by 40 armed riders. One of the riders walked into the priest's house, announcing the arrival of McDougall's messenger. Riel greeted Provencher at the door, smiling at the man as he extended his hand in friendship.

"I welcome you, Monsieur. What news from Pembina?"

Provencher was led into the house where John Bruce, Father Ritchot and a few other Métis were sitting around a table. More than a little disconcerted at being in the presence of so many armed Métis, Provencher stammered heavily when he spoke.

"Why is the governor being kept from entering this territory?"

Louis Riel put on his most diplomatic voice. "Please don't misunderstand me, Monsieur Provencher. I do not doubt that McDougall would do everything in his power to protect and promote the rights of the English-speaking settlers living in this community. What I am worried about are the rights of my own people. Everything we have seen about the Canadians to this time suggests that they deem our presence here as nothing but an inconvenience to their own ambitions." Riel looked around at men sitting around him before continuing. "It is my goal to set up a democratically elected government on the Red River, a body which will allow the Métis to legally negotiate with the Canadians because I doubt that Monsieur McDougall will do this on our behalf."

Louis' genteel tone surprised Provencher, who noted the contrast between the careful manners of the man in front of him and the heavily armed Métis who had led him here. It struck him then that it was up to his government which Métis face they would deal with: the plain-speaking man who sat before him, speaking of democracy and rights or the rugged riders outside who did their talking with muskets and revolvers.

Ambroise Lépine (1840–1923), one of the most respected Métis buffalo hunters in Red River, became close friends with Riel.

"Please believe that you have my sympathies, Monsieur Riel," Provencher responded. "Regardless of how I feel, though, the Dominion government has chosen McDougall for governor. It's the law."

Riel looked away from Provencher, thinking carefully about what the man had just said. "Yes, the government," he muttered, more to himself than anyone in the room, "the law." He turned his attention to the secretary again. "Monsieur Provencher, neither myself nor anyone at this table is adverse to joining Canada; we just want to be sure that it is done according to our own conditions."

With these words, Riel dismissed the messenger, ordering a group of horsemen to escort the man safely back to Pembina. He shook Provencher's hand just before he departed.

"There is no reason we cannot resolve this issue civilly, Monsieur Provencher," Riel said. "All I ask is that my people's rights be respected."

Provencher left Riel's company, profoundly moved by the exchange. Meanwhile, just north of the U.S. border, McDougall was having a far more harrowing experience with the Métis. Having disregarded Riel's order to remain in Pembina, McDougall left the American town right after Provencher departed, setting himself up in a small Hudson's Bay Company fort a stone's throw away from the border. Apparently, even this insignificant advance north was too much. On November 2, 50 armed horsemen, led by National Committee Adjutant-General Ambroise Lépine, descended on McDougall's little party, escorting the would-be governor's little party back to the United States. A blustering, sputtering McDougall held up his government commission before Lépine, but the laconic buffalo hunter was unmoved.

McDougall then tried to convey a noble indignation as Métis strongmen moved to put him in his wagon.

"Who has ordered this outrage?" demanded McDougall. "I swear the responsible parties will pay!"

"The government," was Lépine's short reply.

Lépine's band escorted McDougall to the border, where Lépine rode up to McDougall's coach. His parting words to McDougall were short but cut deep.

"If you cross this line again," the buffalo hunter stated matter-of-factly, "you will be put under arrest." With these words, Lépine wheeled his mount and headed back north, leaving McDougall to trudge back to Pembina.

So it was that instead of being enthroned as "King of the North-West," McDougall was forced to rely on the good grace of a Half-breed named William Hallet, who allowed McDougall and his retinue to stay in his humble log cabin. Along with the original inhabitants of the log home, McDougall's party of 18 people was crammed into the small space just as winter began to settle on the prairies. He was interviewed by a visiting American journalist who was taken by the idea of a governor of a territory living in such squalor.

"A king without a kingdom is said to be poorer than a peasant," the cheeky journalist quipped after talking with McDougall. "Certainly, it is a spectacle sufficiently sad to move the hardest heart."

If there were those who thought relegating the North-West's future governor to frontier poverty for an entire winter was going too far, Louis Riel was about to demonstrate that he intended to go a lot further. On the morning of November 2, small groups of Métis began trickling into Fort Garry inconspicuously, affecting everyday business and conversation. They were armed, but that was not terribly unusual in the Red River region, where revolvers and rifles were as common as hats and boots. There was no cause to suspect anything, until, that is, Dr. William Cowan, the chief factor at the Hudson's Bay Company fort, looked up from his work to see that 120 armed Métis were suddenly standing inside his fort's walls. Louis Riel stood at their head. It didn't require a doctor to surmise that something was up, and the perturbed factor strode up to Riel demanding to know his business.

"Good morning to you, Dr. Cowan," Riel began, offering his hand in greeting. The chief factor ignored Louis' outstretched hand, but Riel's cordial tone did not change a bit. "We've come to guard the fort."

Cowan looked at Riel darkly.

"Against whom?" he rumbled at the Métis leader.

Riel puffed himself up for the response. "Against a danger, my good doctor, which I have reason to believe threatens it, but which I cannot explain to you at this time." Riel had reasons for being evasive.

Fort Garry, just south of Winnipeg, was the hub of the entire settlement: a crucial economic center, where all the region's roads converged at the Hudson's Bay Company. Moreover, with its high walls, cannons and extensive armory, it was easily defensible, making it a key strategic location in the Red River region. What if the Hudson's Bay Company were to abruptly close off the fort, enlisting a few supporters to garrison it? Worse, what if Schultz's faction seized it? Rumors to that effect, which were later confirmed to be true, had been circulating in the community for some time. Under Riel's leadership, the Métis acted decisively. Moved to action by the possibility that Fort Garry would be taken by hostile forces, the Métis staged a preemptive occupation of the important site.

Still, Riel knew that such an occupation would be seen by many as an overly aggressive move, and he understood the danger of leaning too heavily on military strength as a basis for leadership. He knew that Ottawa would accept the legitimacy of his government only if it was democratically appointed. And so it was that the ever-energetic Métis leader promptly began dialogue to establish a more formal government. In an effort to address the concerns of the alarmed English-speaking settlers and the more conservative among the Métis population, Riel issued a "Public Notice to the Inhabitants of Rupert's Land," which appeared throughout Red River in early November. The announcement read:

> The President of the French-speaking population of Rupert's Land in council (the invaders of our rights being now expelled), already aware of your sympathy, do extend the hand of friendship to you, our friendly fellow inhabitants. And in so doing, invite you to send 12 Representatives in order to form one body with the above council, which also consists of 12 members, to consider the present political state of the country and to adopt such measures as may be deemed best for the future welfare of the same.

There was some debate among the English-speaking settlers, but they eventually chose to accept the Métis invitation. Two important meetings resulted. The first, on November 16, began badly. The French, ecstatic that their English neighbors had accepted the invitation, welcomed the representatives with a salutary salvo fired off into the sky. It was genuinely well intentioned, though perhaps not the most sagacious move so soon after the Métis had flexed their muscles in the occupation of Fort Garry. Many of the English were upset at what they viewed as an attempt by the French to intimidate them with a show of force.

Still, the two sides sat down around the negotiating table, where it quickly became obvious that the meeting would be a contest between the most influential English representative, James Ross, and Louis Riel. Ross and the English objected to the treatment of McDougall. Riel maintained that it was unfortunate, but necessary. The English proposed that the newly enlarged body should elect a new chairman and secretary, thus threatening to replace Riel and Bruce. Riel refused until the English and French had achieved a broader consensus.

Then Ross played his ace in the hole. Governor Mactavish, under pressure from McDougall and the Canadians, had written a proclamation that described the recent Métis actions as "unlawful acts." In the letter, Mactavish begged the perpetrators of these "crimes" to immediately disperse or suffer "the pains and penalties of law."

Mactavish's messenger read the letter out in front of the entire assembly, every word from the messenger's mouth sending Riel's legitimacy one step closer to the political precipice.

"You are dealing with a crisis out of which may come incalculable good or immeasurable evil," the letter concluded. "And with all the weight of my official authority, and all the influence of my individual position, let me finally charge you to adopt only such means that are lawful and constitutional, rational and safe."

Ross rose immediately and tried to capitalize on the impact of the letter, claiming Mactavish's document was proof that the Métis

Upper Fort Garry, established by the Hudson's Bay Company; a key supply center for its fur-trading operation in Rupert's Land

were in a state of rebellion. He then seconded a motion that Métis lay down their arms and quit Fort Garry.

Mactavish was a well-respected figure and his words carried significant weight in the community. The French representatives at the table were taken aback, but Riel quickly found his feet. The flushed Métis leader sprang from his chair.

"If we are rebels," he replied, his voice shaking with emotion, "we are rebels against the company that sold us and is ready to hand us over, enemies against those who believe our rights can be purchased! We are not in rebellion against the British Crown, which has not yet given its approval for the final transfer of the country."

Thus, Riel deftly incorporated Ross' criticism of the Métis rebellion into the grievances of exclusion that were commonly held by French and English alike. But he was not finished.

"Moreover," he said, looking each delegate square in the eyes, "we are true to our native land. We are protecting it against dangers that threaten it. We wish the people of Red River to be a free people. Let us help one another. Let us remain shoulder to shoulder. We all heard the words of Mr. Mactavish. He says that out of this meeting and its decision may come incalculable good. Let us unite. If we are strong, the evil that he fears will not come to pass. Hear how he speaks. Is it surprising? His children are Half-breeds like ourselves."

It was a fine display of rhetoric and quick-witted politicking. Riel used Mactavish's words to turn what looked like certain defeat into sudden victory.

"Everyone I have seen agrees in saying that Louis Riel surpassed himself in the preliminary debates," a parish representative named Father Lestanc later wrote, "and that he flattened James Ross."

The second meeting, held on November 23, became bogged down in more debate between Ross and Riel. They argued all day and into the night, but nothing was decided. Louis was reflecting on the futility of the second day's debate after the meeting had ended. He decided that to break open the deadlock he would present the representatives with a bold, new strategy: they would replace the moribund Council of Assiniboia and the recently established National Committee with a formally elected provisional government, which would have the power to negotiate with the Hudson's Bay Company and the Dominion government.

The committee members considered this a radical move, and Riel had difficulty convincing his own people that forming a provisional government was the right thing to do. Riel could hardly believe the opposition he had to face from his French-speaking brethren. His compatriots feared that the formation of a sovereign government would be construed as rebellion against the Queen. He only managed to sell the idea by stressing that such a governing body wasn't a petulant strike against the British Crown, but a necessary substitution for the now impotent Council of Assiniboia.

The following day, when Ross again demanded to know what the French *really* wanted, Riel met him head on with a body of united Métis representatives behind him.

"I believe we want what every French parish wants, indeed, what Red River needs to survive," the Métis leader said. "It is of our opinion that we should form a provisional government, a democratic authority that will serve for our protection and lend us a legitimate voice to negotiate with Canada."

Louis took a long look at the English delegates before him.

"In all sincerity, we invite you to join in it. God willing, this government will be made up equally of French and English."

It was a bold proposition. Ross' party, either surprised by Louis' willingness to give the minority English exactly half the seats in the government, or perhaps agreeing with the clear direction of his reasoning, was finally inclined to side with Riel.

Meanwhile, McDougall schemed a plan of his own. The appointed lieutenant-governor, still held up on the American border, was not at all happy. He had managed, at least, to have a log cabin built to serve as a crude base of operations for himself and his staff. But there was little room in this tiny administrative office on the border for McDougall's throne *and* his ego. A month hadn't elapsed before the exiled ruler of Rupert's Land was considering a premature return to Ottawa. If not for the encouragement from a few men in the Red River community, McDougall would have probably quit his ambitions in the North-West. Mair and Snow had written him, feeding his waning hopes, urging that he should not depart. The day would soon enough be theirs, they assured him.

"The English have not yet risen," the letters promised, with all the insidiousness of the Biblical serpent. "They only wait for the call, and they will rise to support you, their rightful leader."

Associating with Schultz's faction was damaging to McDougall's reputation in Canada's prospective colony. Even Prime Minister Macdonald recognized that they were "indiscreet" and "offensive." Upon learning of the situation in Red River, the prime minister warned McDougall against fraternization with Schultz's gang.

"You must bridle those gentlemen," Macdonald wrote to his appointee, "or they will be a continual source of disquiet to you."

Instead, McDougall placed his trust in the ragtag band of bigots, thus quashing whatever hopes he still entertained of assuming his kingly position.

The date of the scheduled transfer of Rupert's Land to Canada was fast approaching, and McDougall, waiting for word on what to do next from his superiors in Ottawa, heard nothing. He became desperate. What to do? If McDougall did nothing, and the governance of the Hudson's Bay Company expired with no other authority to replace it, then the region would be, de facto, without a government. It was an established principle of international law that, in such a case, the people of Red River would have the right to form their own government to maintain order and mete out justice. Macdonald made it a point to remind McDougall of this fact in several letters.

Apparently, a legitimate, justified government of and for the people of Red River was a possibility that McDougall wished to avoid at all costs. So, antsy and uninformed in Pembina, McDougall took a desperate gamble. On December 1, 1869, McDougall set out from Pembina. Bundled against the howling wind and driving snow, he clutched a forged Royal Proclamation in his hands. In a bizarre political ceremony performed for his benefit alone, the spurned governor trudged up to the Canadian border and shouted the Queen's right to the land into an indifferent wind. From that instant on, as far as McDougall was concerned, Rupert's Land and all that inhabited it were his. The forged proclamation was then smuggled through to the ever-helpful John Schultz, who quickly printed up hundreds of copies and plastered them all over the settlement.

McDougall's underhanded tactic was doomed. The fact that he declared ownership of Rupert's Land with a forged Royal Proclamation would not have come back to haunt him if the Hudson's Bay Company actually ceded Rupert's Land to the Dominion government on December 1, as initially agreed upon. But unbeknownst to all in the North-West, Prime Minister Macdonald, nervous about the Métis unrest, decided to delay the land transfer.

On November 27, Canada's governor general had wired the Colonial Office in London, curtly stating, "Canada cannot accept transfer unless quiet possession is given." Out of the loop in Pembina, McDougall had yet to hear the news.

At first, the news of McDougall's proclamation had the desired effect. When the convention of English and French representatives reconvened on December 1, support from the English for a provisional government had wavered noticeably. Riel seemed to be the only one who suspected McDougall's proclamation might be phony.

"If Mr. McDougall really is our governor today," Riel addressed the assembly with measured skepticism, "then our chances at rightful recognition are better than ever. He has no more to do than prove to us his desire to treat us well. If he guarantees our rights, I will be one of those who go to meet him and escort him as far as the seat of his government."

When Ross and the English pressed Riel as to what, exactly, these "rights" were, Louis was ready. Riel presented the assembled representatives with his prepared List of Rights. It spelled out requirements for a more democratic and bilingual government, tackled the common concern of land title, required that the Dominion negotiate treaties with nearby Native tribes to ensure a lasting peace on the frontier and even demanded that the Canadian government offer the colony material support and federal representation. The list was accepted by all, and why not? Generous and fair, the catalog of demands addressed the concerns of all parties. It was another political coup for Riel, who had again conjured consolidation in the Red River settlements through a proposal of bold inclusiveness.

But then, just as it appeared the situation was resolved, the delegates unexpectedly came to an impasse again. Now that their rights were spelled out and agreed upon, the English demanded that McDougall be admitted unconditionally and without further delay. This appeared sheer folly to the French, who prudently insisted that McDougall be allowed to enter the settlement only after guaranteeing that he and the Canadian government would abide by the agreed-upon rights.

As the debate flared, so did Riel's temper. He could not understand why the English were threatening to scrap all the hard-bargained progress he thought they had just achieved. For the first time in his short political career, Louis Riel lost his temper.

"Go return peacefully to your farms!" he finally exploded at the English. "Stay in the arms of your wives. Give this example to your children," he chided. "But watch us act. We are going ahead to work and obtain the guarantee of our rights and yours. You will come to share them in the end."

Riel's caution would eventually be justified when it was discovered that McDougall's "Royal Proclamation" was indeed a forgery. In the meantime, however, on the cusp of a historic agreement, the negotiations between French and English settlers on the Red River thudded to a frustrating and nerve-wracking halt.

Perhaps Riel's fuse was shortened by an even more flagrant blunder committed by McDougall. He named the government surveyor, Colonel Dennis, "Conservator of the Peace," and, no doubt reacting to a fear that the Métis might resist his rule, authorized Dennis to "raise, organize, arm, equip and provision a sufficient force to attack, arrest, fire upon, pull down or break into any fort, house or stronghold." McDougall knew full well that his authority rested on nothing more than a forged document, but with determination falling somewhere between bravery and stupidity, he went ahead and commissioned a police force for the Red River settlement.

Dennis made his way across the border and went to work. He recruited only among the enemies of the French: Half-breeds who were opposed to Riel's movement and the traditional Native rivals of the Métis, the Salteaux and the Sioux. By December 5, Dennis had 380 Indians, Half-breeds and Canadians training in the abandoned stone fort about 20 miles north of the settlement.

The more established English-speaking residents refused to have anything to do with such foolishness, but Schultz and a group of his henchmen eagerly sledded up to Dennis' impromptu headquarters. They were ready and willing to lead the charge into the French parishes themselves, as they pointedly informed McDougall's illegitimate military commander. Dennis was not quite so stupid. For while he had mustered almost 400 men, the colonel had acquired only 200 guns, and too many of these were old and barely functional. With his force, better equipped with zeal than weaponry, Dennis was supposed to march 20 miles to the south and attack a strongly garrisoned Fort Garry equipped with cannons in the middle of winter?

"Go back to your homes and stay there until otherwise instructed," Dennis rebuffed Schultz and his men. "In the meantime, do not in any way provoke the Métis."

Maybe Schultz's subsequent course of action might be explained by his failure to understand what Dennis meant by "not in any way." Or perhaps he thought a sufficient provocation would force Dennis' hand and bring him rushing to Schutlz's aid. In any case, immediately after returning to Winnipeg, Schultz and his supporters began transforming his part-brick house and store into what would soon be dubbed "Fort Schultz."

Riel, at first, tried a gentle and reasonable approach, writing Schultz a note to warn him against this aggression. To no one's surprise, the message was ignored, and the "garrison" at "Fort Schultz" continued to entrench.

So it was that Schultz and his boys promptly managed to break Colonel Dennis' explicit order to "not in any way provoke the French Half-breeds." On December 2, in the face of impending civil war, Riel shut down both Schultz's *Nor'Wester* and James Ross' *Red River Pioneer*. As well, he temporarily confiscated all weapons and ammunition for sale in the town of Winnipeg.

On December 6 the Métis watching "Fort Schultz" captured two men, Alexander McArthur and Thomas Scott, who were trying to run the gauntlet in order to reach the old stone fort, where Colonel Dennis was still stationed. The standoff grew even tenser the next day, when Riel managed to get his hands on a copy of McDougall's foolishly provocative authorization for Dennis to raise an army. Calling together every Métis fighting man he could, Riel read the document to the assembled soldiers to give them an idea of what kind of people they were up against. After he read it, he tore the inflammatory order to shreds, letting the pieces scatter onto the snow.

"These are the sort of men we are dealing with," Louis called to those assembled before him. "Remember these words, and be careful not to underestimate their ability for violence." So motivated, 300 Métis troops moved out to Schultz's home-cum-stronghold, with two cannons from Fort Garry in tow. A bristling ring of cannon and rifle now surrounded Schultz's flimsy fortress. There were few who doubted what the outcome would be if it came to shooting.

Things could have gotten quite ugly if it were not for Andrew Bannatyne. Hoping to avert bloodshed, Riel agreed to allow the established and well-liked English Half-breed to mediate between the forces. The ever-intransigent Schultz looked down his nose at Bannatyne, demanding that Riel agree to a list of his demands before his men would consider surrender. Riel looked incredulously at Bannatyne when the Half-breed relayed the demands.

"Doesn't he see the situation he's in?" Louis asked, bewildered. "We have him surrounded and hopelessly outgunned. This man is in no position to be making demands."

Riel stonily refused any concession, replying only with a demand that Schultz and his followers surrender unconditionally.

Every man, woman and child who surveyed the standoff from outside knew that Schultz's men would be slaughtered if they chose to fight. After a few days, this realization began to sink in with the men inside. They had backed themselves into a lethal corner. John O'Donnel, a doctor from Minnesota who had accompanied McDougall westward, was the first to crack. Moments after he walked out of Schultz's home, arms in the air, the entire rabble, Schultz included, was suddenly cured of its military delusions and quickly followed suit. The lone exception was Charlie Mair, perhaps poetically immune to such realism, who was still demanding the Canadians fight to his idea of a noble death.

The demoralized Canadians filed out of the house and were immediately surrounded by armed Métis, who marched them straight down main street and into the waiting jail cells at Fort Garry. The Métis fired a celebratory volley into the night sky, humiliating the helpless gang that Schultz had led astray.

Yet in their defeat, Schultz's men had ironically succeeded in one respect: their vain standoff had provoked Colonel Dennis to action. On December 9, Dennis issued a peace proclamation, commanding all of his men and would-be recruits to stand down. With that, McDougall's appointed commander exhibited resourcefulness on top of sound judgment and hightailed it back to Pembina disguised as an old Native woman.

McDougall, too, finally quit the field, his once-sweet dreams of wealth and power in the North-West now nothing but a bitter, taunting memory. His political career was in ruins.

CHAPTER THREE

Intrigue

THE OVERLY ZEALOUS DRIVE of Schultz's faction, coupled with the poorly organized efforts of the Canadian government, left the French community in Red River more united than ever. Riel knew political momentum when he saw it. With the assistance of Father Georges Dugas and Father Noel-Joseph Ritchot, Louis worked through the entire night following Schultz's surrender to draft a proclamation that aimed to justify the Métis' actions to date and express their movement's future intentions. The "Declaration of the People of Rupert's Land and the North-West" appeared throughout Red River in French and English the following day.

A lofty rhetorical work, the document railed against McDougall's despotic ambitions and the hostile Canadian rabble that followed him. Riel, Ritchot and Dugas also derided Ottawa's assumption that the Dominion government had a right to Rupert's Land and its subjects and argued that the government had effectively denied Red River residents their rights as British subjects. Riel and the two priests didn't mince words when they stated that the Métis would resist any rule by force of arms.

Nevertheless, the declaration affirmed that the Métis were willing to enter negotiations with the Dominion government if it was done through proper channels—meaning through the Métis provisional government, a body that derived its legitimacy through the "obedience and respect of its subjects." Moreover, since Ottawa's authority was considered illegitimate, and the Hudson's Bay Company had relinquished control in its botched sale of Rupert's Land, the formation of the provisional government wasn't only legitimate, but *necessary* in the political vacuum left behind by the Council of Assiniboia's dissolution. After all, there had to be *some* governing power to enforce law and protect property. Thus, it was stated in the Declaration that the provisional government was officially born on November 24, 1869, the day the Hudson's Bay Company signed away its rights to the North-West.

The declaration was met with widespread support in the Métis parishes, and after Mass at St. Boniface on Friday, December 10, 1869, Riel announced the establishment of the provisional government to a cheering congregation.

"Let word be spread that today shall be a holiday, to celebrate the birth of a government for the Métis!"

"What of the English?" one of the parishioners shouted, asking about the English-speaking Half-breeds and the Selkirk settlers to the north. "Do they stand with us?"

"Not yet," Riel responded gravely. "We haven't been able to come to an agreement with our English-speaking brethren, but rest assured, we are working on it."

This was a detail the Métis were willing to overlook for the time being. Eager to have something to celebrate, the assembled parishioners made their way to Fort Garry in cheerful procession, gathering everyone they met along the way. They congregated in the open courtyard of Fort Garry where the Métis flag was run up the fort flagpole. A sudden breeze caught the banner and the emblem of the *fleur de lis* and shamrock unfurled, snapping sharply in the wind. Riel then addressed the Métis before him, delivering an exuberant speech that roused the Métis in a way that only he was able. When he was finished, a festive cheer surged through the crowd, and as the St. Boniface Boys' Bugle Band kicked into a lively tune, all present drew from a great cauldron full of liquor in the center of court-yard. The Métis raised their flagons to join in three hearty toasts: one for the provisional government, one for Louis and one for the band. Meanwhile, Schultz, Mair and their miserable followers could do nothing but watch the flowing unity and goodwill from behind the bars of the Fort Garry jail. Had they known, they might have found some consolation in the fact that this newfound unity was about to be severely tested.

On Christmas Day, Riel was informed that two Canadian emissaries had arrived in Pembina. One was the Reverend Jean-Baptiste Thibault and the other was Colonel Charles de Salaberry. A message from Pembina had been sent ahead of the two by an American speculator named Enos Stutsman, who was friendly to the Métis resistance.

Stutsman had penned a hasty warning to Riel: "If the emissaries are permitted free communication with your people, they will give you trouble. Inasmuch as Father Thibault comes in an official capacity, he should be regarded as a government official and not as a minister of Christ." Events would eventually show that Stutsman's suspicions lent the two Dominion representatives far more pull than they actually possessed.

So it was that Riel had his guard up when the two delegates arrived in Red River. He had the two placed under house arrest on arrival and confiscated all the documents they were carrying. Louis wanted to be sure he knew exactly what he was dealing with in these two Québec diplomats. Riel quickly came to realize that neither Thibault nor de Salaberry would do much harm. Both men carried documents indicating that the Dominion government was thoroughly embarrassed by events of the previous months. A letter from Secretary of State for the Provinces Joseph Howe disavowed the "acts of folly and indiscretion which had been committed by persons purporting to represent the Dominion" and offered an amnesty to all Métis who would disarm and avoid further action against Ottawa. As comforting as this conciliatory offer might have been, it was offset by a certain degree of frustration on Riel's part. He was soon to learn that these two men were only "goodwill ambassadors," sent to smooth over relations with the Métis. They possessed no real power to negotiate. Deeming them harmless, Riel released the pair from house arrest.

Donald Smith, the third Canadian agent to arrive from Ottawa, was another story. If Riel had known what sort of mischief Smith would cause in the Red River, he would have locked him up and thrown away the key. A clenched fist in a velvet glove, the outwardly affable Donald Smith was sent to Red River by John A. Macdonald, ostensibly to assist the tubercular William Mactavish in his administration of the territory. His real mission, however, was to foment dissent against Louis Riel. It was a smart move on the prime minister's part. Smith was the chief factor of the Hudson's Bay Company in the Montréal district, and the many Métis with strong ties to the company knew him well. Macdonald was right in assuming that Smith could garner support for the region's former administration, and he couldn't have found a better man for the job.

If the Métis are reminded of their old loyalties to the Hudson's Bay Company, Macdonald thought, *then they will be more likely to recognize the transfer of sovereignty to the Dominion government.*

A rugged man of nearly 50 years, Donald Smith was imbued with that robust frontier charisma that many Métis recognized and responded to. With his sparse, short-cropped hair, thick gnarly beard and big red eyebrows that threatened to grow over his no-nonsense gaze, Smith could have easily been mistaken for a Métis. But underneath this tough exterior was a mind of cold calculation and ruthless cunning.

Riel knew that Smith was a senior administrator, so the Métis leader didn't have too much difficulty buying Smith's story that he had been sent to help the bedridden Mactavish. Nevertheless, Riel

Donald Smith (1820–1914) in 1894, whose political maneuverings came close to thwarting the Métis Resistance.

was wary, and he ordered that Smith not be allowed to leave Fort Garry while he was in Red River. He also made Smith promise that he would do nothing to undermine the provisional government.

Although undermining the provisional government was precisely what the prime minister had sent Smith to do, the slick administrator told Riel that he did not intend to do any such thing. Almost the very moment Riel turned his back, Smith went to work.

Not permitted to leave Fort Garry, Smith made use of his contacts through the local Hudson's Bay infrastructure, and it was not long before Red River residents were lining up to see him. Some of them came out of a residual loyalty for the company; others were motivated by a deep-seated dislike for Louis Riel, his regime and how it interfered with their interests; the rest came for the federal handouts.

Smith was armed with more than his title and his charisma. Macdonald had also made provision for human corruption and informed Smith that he was to spare no expense in bribing any Red River resident into joining his camp. Poverty-stricken Métis proved to be just as susceptible to greenback persuasion as their English counterparts, and Smith unloaded hundreds of pounds sterling on the frontier inhabitants. His most valuable convert was a prominent Métis named Charles Nolin, who served as a member of the provisional government and was one of Riel's cousins. The mercurial Nolin was driven by ambitions that far outstripped his abilities, and he had become cursed with an envious bitterness when Riel took up the political reins of the region. It was easy for Smith to entice him into the dissenter's camp. With Nolin's help, Smith began to exceed Macdonald's expectations, courting significant numbers of English, Scottish and Métis away from Riel. Along with Nolin, Smith managed to bank another two councillors in the provisional government. The pull of Smith's bottomless pockets was sending ripples through the community.

Riel didn't know how much damage Smith had done until it was too late. Even as Smith was bribing everyone he could against the provisional government, he was also telling Louis Riel that his influence back east reached into the halls of Parliament.

"We need to talk sometime," he would say to the Métis leader. "You know, the prime minister isn't necessarily *averse* to what you're doing here. He's actually a very reasonable man."

Smith always said just enough to keep Riel coming back. And it was only when Louis, tired of Smith's smoke and mirrors, acted to find out exactly how much authority the Hudson's Bay chief factor brought with him from Ottawa, that he found out how powerful his adversary had become.

Donald Smith knew that his two predecessors, Thibault and de Salaberry, had been stripped of their official papers when they arrived in the region, so he took measures to safeguard his own, leaving his documents with McDougall's former secretary, A.N. Provencher, who was still living in Pembina. When Louis learned of this, he had three Métis riders go down to Pembina to seize Smith's credentials. By this time, Smith had eyes and ears all over the region, and when he was told of Riel's efforts, he sent his own cadre of Half-breeds to Pembina. Smith's party got there first, nabbing the chief factor's papers from Provencher and promptly heading back north to Fort Garry.

Riel and Father Ritchot rode out to St. Norbert with Donald Smith in tow. Riel and Ritchot were confident that three Métis would be waiting for them with Smith's documents, but instead, found themselves facing Smith's gang, who handed over the papers to their rightful owner. Things almost got very ugly. One of Smith's riders, a man named Pierre Léveillé, harbored an especially virulent dislike for Louis Riel and his Métis movement. Boiling over in anger, Léveillé threw Father Ritchot out of his way, shouting something about how priests would do best to stay in their churches. He then pulled his revolver and trained it on Louis Riel.

"Give me one reason I shouldn't blow this rabble-rouser away right now," Léveillé growled to no one in particular.

Riel's life may have been cut short then and there if not for Smith's intervention.

"Put that thing away!" the chief factor roared. "The last thing I need is a martyr on my hands!" Smith then turned to Riel and spoke with all the kindness he could muster. "Mr. Riel, I'm sorry for this, but I have been charged to present the contents of these papers to the Red River population. They are not for your eyes alone."

Riel looked at Smith with complete resignation. "What would you have me do?"

"Call a public meeting at Fort Garry on January 19. I will announce the purpose of my mission in Red River on that date." With these words, Smith and his party turned their horses around and galloped back to the fort, leaving Riel and Ritchot standing in the bitter winter cold.

The seasons seemed to be in tune with Riel's difficulties. As the sun skimmed just over the barren horizon for but a few hours daily, dark times settled in for the Métis resistance. On January 9, Charlie Mair, along with his hotheaded new friend Thomas Scott and several others imprisoned at Fort Garry managed a jailbreak. They had been whittling away at the window casings in their cells for days with concealed knives and had finally done enough damage to break free. During a changing of the guard, the Canadians made their move and slipped away into the night. Five were recaptured the next day, but Mair and Scott managed to make their way through the deathly cold to the relative safety of Portage la Prairie, home to many of the recently arrived Canadian settlers and an English enclave in the Red River region. The jailbreak was demoralizing enough for Louis' camp, but the resistance still had farther to fall.

Smith's public meeting took place in the courtyard of Fort Garry 10 days after the small group of Canadians made their escape. Riel had thought of ignoring Smith's demand for a meeting on that day but knew the matter was out of his hands when it became obvious how much support the chief factor had behind him. It was a request he couldn't refuse.

They came crowding into the fort on the 19th, despite the vicious winter cold. By snowshoe, sled and foot, men, women and children from all over the settlement made the arduous journey to hear what Donald Smith had to say. On the gallery of the stone corporate offices facing the open courtyard that was packed with snow and spectators stood the key actors in the drama: Donald Smith and Louis Riel. Riel was there as Smith's translator. The two were joined by Judge Black, who had agreed to act as the formal secretary for the public meeting, and the English Half-breed Thomas Bunn, who chaired the proceedings.

Smith set the tone for the meeting by beginning with an objection to the Métis flag that fluttered over the assembly. His opening statements were received in a silence colder than the brittle surrounding air. Sensing the tension in the air, Smith realized that he wasn't as popular as he had thought, and so continued on with a little more caution. Opening the satchel he was carrying, Smith pulled out his papers and began to read. He began with a letter that Secretary of State for the Provinces Joseph Howe had sent him, asking that he go to Red River to win over the settlement to Canada. Next, the Hudson's Bay agent read another piece of correspondence, this one from the Canadian governor general, Sir John Young. The governor general wrote that the Queen was upset by the happenings in Red River but was willing to listen to the grievances of her subjects. The governor general himself promised amnesty to all those who would lay down their arms and cease their resistance.

"You see?" Smith said to the gathered settlers after he had finished reading the final letter. "Not everyone from the East is as harsh, intemperate and dishonest as the men you've encountered so far." Riel translated Smith's words into French. The Métis absorbed the message in thoughtful silence

"Mr. McDougall"—a series of boos and catcalls erupted at Smith's mention of the area's intended governor—"erred greatly in his actions." The crowd fell silent again. "None in Ottawa or London agree with his actions, and he will never come back to this region again. I implore you, put down your weapons and cooperate with Ottawa's purchase. These are the wishes of the Hudson's Bay Company, the Dominion government and the Queen." Smith's supporters in the crowd were bolstered by the speech.

"Release the prisoners!" the voice of John Burke, a Half-breed in Smith's camp, rang from the courtyard. Most of the Métis in the fort turned and glared, believing such a suggestion to be premature.

"Not yet," Riel responded from the gallery.

"Yes," came the excited reply from another of Smith's supporters somewhere in the crowd, "they must be released!"

A rowdy hubbub ensued, and people pressed forward towards the stage. If not for the presence of a cordon of armed Métis buffalo hunters that quickly surrounded Riel, things may have taken an ugly turn. A full-blown riot was deterred only under the threat of leveled rifle barrels.

It was a low point for the resistance, but it also proved to be a catalyst for action. Father Lestanc and Father Thibault—the same Father Thibault who had preceded Smith as an emissary from the East— weren't happy with Smith's bribe-based support. When the chief factor's actions pushed the settlement to the brink of violence and possibly even civil war, the pair decided that it was time for some divine intervention. Lestanc and Thibault made their rounds in the community on the evening of the 19th, speaking in favor of peace and Louis Riel. Their efforts were not wasted on the religious inhabitants.

The following day, another meeting was called, and Reverend Henry Cockran stepped onto the platform and offered to translate the proceedings into Cree, a conciliatory gesture to the Indians present.

John Burke stepped forward and, clearing his throat, spoke to the assembled crowd. "I have a confession to make, my friends. The words I spoke yesterday were not my own, but put to me by *another party* to say. I am ashamed to admit that I was so easily influenced." One did not need powers of clairvoyance to discern who Burke's "other party" was.

Then Father Lestanc rose and addressed the reassembled crowd with a broad smile. "We have been good friends to this day in the whole settlement," he said in his mildest voice, "and I want to certify here that we will be good friends tonight." The entire gathering broke into a rousing cheer, the rancor sown by Smith withering on the vine.

Still, Smith tried to regain his momentum from the previous day. He began by reading more of the letters he had brought with him from Ottawa. It was laborious stuff, and the often wordy, bureaucratic text wasn't aided any by his monotone delivery. People shuffled to stay warm, rubbed gloved hands together and hunched low into deep collars. Smith could see that he was losing the audience in the dropping wind chill, and broke off into an off-the-cuff and more personal appeal.

"My friends, I beg you to remember that I am no outsider to this community. My wife is Isabella Hardisty, whose family goes back generations on the Red River. I feel no slight responsibility for the outcome of this conflict and sincerely hope that my humble efforts may in some measure contribute to bring about a peaceable union and entire accord among all classes of the people of this land," he finished.

If Smith's emotional plea drew some applause from those assembled, it was half-hearted, at best. That was when Louis Riel stepped forward, intent on taking advantage of Smith's suddenly flagging support. Drawing himself up to his full height, Riel let a few dramatic moments pass before he spoke.

"I agree wholeheartedly with Mr. Smith," he began, his sonorous words gathering everyone's undivided attention as they rolled through the fort. "I, too, wish for union and entire accord among all classes and people of this land. This is precisely why I have been arguing for a united voice for our people."

Murmurs ran through the crowd.

"To establish such a voice, we need an organized body of representatives." Riel emphasized his next words. "You must believe me when I say that neither I nor any Métis in the Red River has any wish to exclude our English brothers from such a body. Their voices have as much right to be heard as ours." A few shouts of encouragement sounded from the courtyard. "That is why I propose an elected convention of exactly 40 delegates, 20 English and 20 French. It would be this body, rather than the staunch sentiments and good graces of Mr. Smith and his Canadian government, that would decide what is best for the welfare of the country. Let us not offer ourselves up to the whims of others. Let us be bold enough to take our fate in our own hands."

A sudden roar of approval erupted from the crowd below, and tears welled up in Louis' eyes. He continued, "I do not wish to keep you in this cold for too much longer, but before we go to the fires of our homes, I would like to express my pride and my love for the people and the land that we call our own. I confess I came here today with a great many fears. Though we are not enemies, English and French and Native among us, it strikes me that we came very near to being so.

"Yet as soon as we understood each other, we decided to join in demanding our just and common rights. I am not afraid to say *our* rights, for each and every one of us has them. They have come to call us 'Half-breeds.' So be it. We accept our title, but let us make it clear that we will take no half-rights. We demand all the rights that we are entitled to. These are the rights that will be set forth by our representatives. These are the rights that I swear to do all I can, and more, to ensure we acquire."

Up on the pulpit, Riel had managed to turn the dissidence and despair infused into the population during the previous day into a collective, newfound optimism. Buoyed by fresh hope, the joyous Métis threw their caps to the sky as Riel finished the last words of his speech. Thunderous cheers were carried across the barren prairie by a frigid January wind, and men who had stood at odds with each other only one day before clasped hands in conciliatory embraces.

Somehow, under the auspices of the Church and Riel's passionate words, the Red River united. Riel hadn't completely discredited Donald Smith in the eyes of the community, but with one speech he had devastated his influence. As a further gesture of goodwill, Riel ordered most of the Métis soldiers to disband and return to their homes. But as it turned out, he was a little too caught up in the relief and elation that swept through the settlement that day.

Three days later, on the night of January 23, another of the Canadian prisoners escaped from Fort Garry. This time, the escapee was none other than John Schultz. The most important and dangerous of the prisoners, Schultz had been imprisoned separately on the top floor of the courthouse jail in Fort Garry. While the Canadian doctor later claimed that his imprisonment had been grim, facts suggest a different story. His wife, Anne, visited him daily and brought him fresh clothes, reading material and home-cooked meals—not exactly the salt mines. In fact, security was so relaxed that Mrs. Schultz was able to hide the means for her husband's eventual escape inside one of her homemade apple brown betties.

Using the penknife so obtained, Schultz cut his buffalo robes into long strips and tied them together into a makeshift rope. Under cover of darkness, Schultz fastened this rope to the window frame, clambered over the sill and began lowering himself down the courthouse wall. He didn't go far before the improvised rope broke, sending Schutlz falling to the snowy ground below. His landing wasn't graceful, and Schultz swallowed his pain-filled curses when he tried to get back on his feet, only to realize that one of his legs was broken. But Schultz was a man of incredible determination, and, gritting his teeth, he limped his way towards one of Fort Garry's exterior walls.

It was one of those frigid Canadian winter nights when open skin immediately feels the pain of exposure, and the coatless Schultz was shaking violently by the time he made it to the wall. At least the extreme cold had drawn the sentries indoors. So it was that the Métis patrol, more concerned with keeping warm than guarding the barren, snow-swept landscape, missed the sight of their captive limping determinedly across the prairie. Schultz did not make it far before the temperature became a lethal impediment. Barely making it to the township of Kildonan, Schultz collapsed in a near-delirious hypothermic heap on the doorstep of a Half-breed named Robert MacBeth.

MacBeth, who had sat on the Council of Assiniboia and so endured more than his fair share of Schultz's lampooning in the *Nor'Wester*, had no great love for the man. On the other hand, turning him in could well have signed Schultz's death warrant. So it was that MacBeth hid Schultz in his attic for two days as Métis soldiers combed the valley with orders to shoot the escapee on sight. Convalescing under MacBeth's care, Schultz eventually was well enough to make his way to the English parish of St. Andrew. He immediately began to foment more trouble.

Riel was livid at the news. He and Lépine delivered such a verbal barrage on the guards that the sheepish men might have preferred to face a cat-o'-nine-tails. The fact that Riel was facing political frustrations once again didn't help his mood. Elections for the convention's representatives had already taken place, and it turned out that his faction had failed to sweep the French parishes. Despite the considerable intervention by the priests, a dissenting French faction led by Charles Nolin—whom everyone knew was still being financed by Donald Smith—had managed to win three of the 20 French seats. It was a small number, but it was more than enough to decisively split the French vote against the 20 English representatives.

The convention's first session, which convened on January 26, 1870, went smoothly enough. Donald Smith continued to plead his case of unconditional cooperation with the Canadian government, rereading his letters of commission from Ottawa, but Red River unity prevailed as delegates made it clear that their body would act as the ultimate authority in the region. The achieved amity prevailed as delegates stood around the Fort Garry council room after the assembly adjourned for the day, shaking hands and patting each other on the back. And Smith must have felt an apprehensive chill at the formal-dress ball that evening, when the invited guests behaved with a noted lack of deference to the once fawned-over man, clearly suggesting their loyalty had been neither rented nor bought by the eastern businessman.

Over the next few days, the convention debated several issues, rewriting the provisional government's original List of Rights to incorporate the concerns of the recently elected English representatives. The new List of Rights was agreed upon with almost no controversy, but problems quickly arose when Donald Smith became involved in the proceedings. Riel, hoping to consolidate the convention's opinions before Smith was allowed to raise his divisive voice, motioned a radical bill—that Red River should enter Canada as a full-fledged province rather than a territory. He argued that a provincial government would have more power than a territorial body, being better able to defend the rights of its residents, and, more importantly, being entitled to greater control over its public lands.

Riel's old opponent, the English representative James Ross, would have nothing to do with this motion.

"A province?" the astounded representative asked, his disbelief speaking for the entire English delegation. "How do you think we could support a full provincial administration? We don't have nearly enough people or resources."

"Yes," the ever-sarcastic Judge John Black chimed in. "I have an idea, why don't we propose to make Winnipeg the new capital of Canada?"

Riel pushed his motion to a vote after the Englishmen's laughter subsided. The Métis lost by three votes. It went exactly as every French representative in the room knew it would: Nolin and the two other Métis on Smith's payroll voted with the English bloc.

Flustered and disappointed, Riel offered another bill, proposing that the sale of the North-West by the Hudson's Bay Company to Canada be declared null and void. The people actually living in the country, and not some foreign power, had the right to negotiate their future, he argued. A valid point, but to try to unilaterally declare the entire agreement brokered between Canada and the Hudson's Bay Company "null and void" was far too radical for the English representatives. This motion, too, failed to pass, with Nolin's small faction again lining up against Riel.

At this point, Louis simply lost his temper. Obviously unable to deal with the second impasse, the Métis leader suddenly rose from his chair and began pacing the courtroom floor, his face flushed with fury. Perhaps Riel was unable to deal with democratic disagreement; maybe he was starting to bend under the pressure of leadership. Or

LIST OF RIGHTS.

1. That the people have the right to elect their own Legislature.

2. That the Legislature have the power to pass all laws local to the Territory over the veto of the Executive by a two-thirds vote.

3. That no act of the Dominion Parliament (local to the Territory) be binding on the people until sanctioned by the Legislature of the Territory.

4. That all Sheriffs, Magistrates, Constables, School Commissioners, etc., be elected by the people.

5. A free Homestead and pre-emption Land Law.

6. That a portion of the public lands be appropriated to the benefit of Schools, the building of Bridges, Roads and Public Buildings.

7. That it be guaranteed to connect Winnipeg by Rail- with the nearest line of Railroad, within a term of five years ; the land grant to be subject to the Local Legislature.

8. That for the term of four years all Military, Civil, and Municipal expenses be paid out of the Dominion funds.

9. That the Military be composed of the inhabitants now existing in the Territory.

10. That the English and French languages be common in the Legislature and Courts, and that all Public Documents and Acts of the Legislature be published in both languages.

11. That the Judge of the Supreme Court speak the English and French languages.

12. That Treaties be concluded and ratified between the Dominion Government and the several tribes of Indians in the Territory to ensure peace on the frontier.

13. That we have a fair and full representation in the Canadian Parliament.

14. That all privileges, customs and usages existing at the time of the transfer be respected.

All the above articles have been severally discussed and adopted by the French and English Representatives without a dissenting voice, as the conditions upon which the people of Rupert's Land enter into Confederation.

The French Representatives then proposed in order to secure the above rights, that a Delegation be appointed and sent to Pembina to see Mr. Macdougall and ask him if he could guarantee these rights by virtue of his commission ; and if he could do so, that then the French people would join to a man to escort Mr. Macdougall into his Government seat. But on the contrary, if Mr. Macdougall could not guarantee such rights, that the Delegates request him to remain where he is, or return 'till the rights be guaranteed by Act of the Canadian Parliament.

The English Representatives refused to appoint Delegates to go to Pembina to consult with Mr. Macdougall, stating, they had no authority to do so from their constituents, upon which the Council was dissolved.

The meeting at which the above resolutions were adopted was held at Fort Garry, on Wednesday, Dec. 1, 1869.
Winnipeg, December 4th, 1869.

The provisional government's List of Rights, drafted by French and English delegates in late January 1870 could Schultz's escape have been nagging at him? Whatever the case, Riel burst into a diatribe.

"The devil take it!" he yelled at the surprised convention. "We must win. The vote may go as it likes; but the will of the Métis must, and will, be carried," he looked squarely at Nolin, "despite those traitorous voices that vote against the good of their people."

That was when Charlie Nolin spoke up. "Monsieur Riel," he responded, "I was not sent here to vote at your dictation. I came here to vote according to my conscience."

"Conscience?" Riel roared back, angrier than ever. "I believe, dear cousin, that your English is failing you. The word you mean to use is avarice."

Riel then turned to the rest of the room, his eyes falling over the English delegates, his voice suddenly controlled, dangerous. "As for the rest of you. When I say this matter must be carried. I mean to say that it *will* be carried. If not here by you, then by the Métis people alone. Do not forget that the Métis provisional government is already in place, and if this convention does not act to protect our rights, then my government will do it regardless."

If Riel could see the hypocrisy of protecting Red River inhabitants' rights while trumping the authority of the elected representatives, he did not show it.

"As for you, Charles Nolin, Tom Harrison and George Klyne," Riel said turning to the three Métis representatives who voted with the English, "your influence as public men is finished in this country! You have lost your influence forever!"

Nolin's dander flared again at this harsh condemnation, and amidst his shouted protests defending his right to vote as he saw fit, the meeting broke up in anxious turmoil.

The events of the previous days—the escape of Schultz, the election of Nolin and his clique, and what Riel viewed as their betrayal at the convention—combined to leave Riel in a foul mood. His anger was directed at the Hudson's Bay Company and those tainted by Smith's tendrils of bribery, trickery and obstruction. The whole community would feel the force of his ire.

Riel and his inner circle of advisors decided to arrest and imprison Charles Nolin. But when the two Métis soldiers sent to carry out the order arrived at Nolin's farm, they discovered that the corrupted representative had gathered a group of armed men. Neither party was willing to back down, and as adrenaline and bravado fed confrontation, two men went for their guns. One was Duncan Nolin, Charles youngest brother, and the other was one of the Métis soldiers sent by Riel. Both men pulled their guns and fired almost simultaneously. As Father Giroux would later state, the "hand of God" interceded, and both guns miraculously misfired. This near bloodshed cooled tempers, and the Métis soldiers rode back to Riel without their prisoner.

This close shave did not deter Riel from continuing his crackdown in Red River. So far he had treated the seriously ill Governor Mactavish—still the official authority in the region—with respect, but the gloves were now off. He surrounded Mactavish's governor's residence with troops, essentially placing him under house arrest. When Dr. William Cowan refused to swear allegiance to the provisional government, Riel publicly went up one side of the chief factor and down the other before having him imprisoned. Riel was so steeled that he even had the affable Andrew Bannatyne imprisoned when the popular Red River resident persisted in his attempts to see Mactavish.

This harder edge certainly spread ripples of apprehension throughout the community. And though Riel had Bannatyne and Cowan released after a few days, and the guard was removed from around Mactavish's residence, the English hadn't missed Riel's message. Nor were they pleased by it. They considered boycotting the next meeting of the convention, but cooler heads eventually prevailed. The English representatives were there when the convention reconvened on February 7, allowing Donald Smith to speak for the first time.

They would witness a historic performance by Riel. He had long suspected that Smith had no real power to negotiate any binding agreements, and he was now relentless with the shifty man, determined to expose him. Smith had only begun to offer his opinion on what the Métis ought to do when Riel interrupted him.

"I am not interested," Riel said, addressing the convention, "in what Mr. Smith thinks but in what he can guarantee. I want some certainty and not merely an expression of opinion on what we desire. Red River has finally attained a position whereby we can make demands. Can the good Hudson's Bay commissioner guarantee them on behalf of the Canadian government?"

Smith was left twisting in the wind.

"While I might have power in regard to some of the articles," the eastern businessman replied, "I have not yet been given any sanction to arrange or enforce any deals between Red River and the government."

The characteristically stoic Smith began to twitch under the collective gaze of the convention.

"You are embarrassed," Riel deadpanned but speaking to Smith. "I see that the Canadian government has not given you all the confidence which they ought to have." Louis was barely able to keep the smile down. "I assure you, Mr. Smith, we hear your opinion, although we are now satisfied that you cannot grant us, nor guarantee us, anything at all."

It was clear to all that Smith had no power to negotiate with the people of Red River. A desperate Smith suggested that the assembly appoint negotiators to deal with Macdonald's government themselves, if they would not deal with him.

This was exactly the kind of opening Riel had been seeking, and he pounced. To whom would the negotiators be responsible, he queried. Who would govern Red River during the negotiations?

"We have arrived at that point, or very near it, where we must consider the nature of this convention," Riel stated. "English and French differences aside, we have been, for the most part, friendly

Louis Riel's closest advisers in 1869. *Top row, left to right:* Charles Larocque, Pierre Delorme, Thomas Bunn, Xavier Pagée, Ambroise Lépine, Baptiste Tourond, Thomas Spence. *Middle row:* Pierre Pointras, John Bruce, Louis Riel, William B. O'Donoghue, François Dauphinais. *Front row:* H.F. O'Lone, Paul Proulx. John Bruce, seated on Louis' right, was the president of the National Committee, but dropped off the political map after he contracted a serious illness. When he recuperated, he found that there was no spot set aside for him in the new provisional government. He never forgave Louis Riel for this perceived slight.

to this point. But we are still bound together in a loose, unsatisfactory way." Riel concentrated especially on the English Half-breeds sitting across from him. "For the good of the community, we must now place ourselves in a more suitable position for discussion. We must," he stressed, "have a more fixed, more established government before proceeding.

"If the convention were to dissolve today," Riel warned the men in the Fort Garry courthouse, "this could very well yield a virtual anarchy, a complete lack of government, which could unleash a flood of distemper and violence over the settlement." Riel looked closely at French- and English-speaker alike. "You know what sort of man this Schultz is, to what lengths he would go to discredit the people here. If we do not act to create a formal provisional government that would represent the whole region now, we might never get the chance again." This was less a threat than a reference. Rumors about the Canadian escapees and their armed and belligerent followers had been flying about the settlement over the previous few days.

Still, the English were hesitant when faced with such a bold step, and debate over what sort of shape the provisional government would take dragged on for two days before Riel lost patience.

"The provisional government is an actual fact," he said to the English delegates after one especially lengthy, cyclic debate. "It has already been established by the Métis. Why not recognize it? We have already done some good by establishing this convention. Let us do more."

The Half-breeds still weren't entirely convinced, and the convention decided to send a formal delegation, two French representatives and two English, to ask Governor Mactavish for his opinion on the matter. Deathly ill, Mactavish barely managed to pull himself up into a sitting position when the four delegates entered his bedchamber. The dying governor did not waste a single breath in his advice.

"Form a government, for God's sake," the tough Scot pronounced, "and restore peace and order in the settlement."

And so it was that Riel won his provisional government. A further committee was formed, which drafted the constitution for the provisional government by February 10. The government was to have a council composed of 12 English and 12 French representatives, with a president, English and French secretaries and a treasurer— equal representation between English and French, although the Métis made up the majority of the population. Louis Riel was appointed president of this new provisional government.

A general celebration erupted as the meeting concluded. "The town welcomed the announcement with a grand display of fireworks and a general and continued discharge of firearms," the *New Nation* reported. In a fitting irony, the fireworks exploding into the windy, snowy night had belonged to John Christian Schultz, having been intended for McDougall's inauguration ceremony. Lit by the multicolored explosions going off in the winter sky, Fort Garry came to life with a lively celebration that lasted into the small hours of the morning. Even Riel, not fond of alcohol, enjoyed a good horn of brandy with the recently released Bannatyne. There were no hard feelings; all acrimony seemed to dissolve in the newfound optimism that spread through Red River. For one night, at least, all was well.

CHAPTER FOUR

Calamity

THE PRECARIOUS ACCORD in Red River was short-lived. For even as the community united under the hard-won provisional government, other forces were mobilizing to tear it down. Discontented residents in the region formed around the vociferous and virulent Canadians who had escaped from Fort Garry in January. From the moment Charlie Mair and Thomas Scott arrived in Portage la Prairie, they began organizing men against Riel. Actually, to call the naysayers who gathered around Mair and Scott an "organization" was a stretch. Between Mair's penchant for romantic dramatization and Scott's near-psychotic hostility towards the Métis, there wasn't much room for any rational organization or expression of opposition. Rather, the motley crew of 60-some English Half-breeds, Salteaux and Sioux that flocked to the Canadian banner in Portage la Prairie was a ragtag gang of armed belligerents who believed their readiness for violence was all the political statement they needed.

On February 9, 1870, one day before Riel's provisional government was formally established, Mair and Scott informed Portage la Prairie's leading citizen, Charles Arkoll Boulton, that they were going to march on Fort Garry to free the men still imprisoned after

Thomas Scott (1842–70) poses for this 1863 photograph, about seven years before he faced a Métis firing squad. Born in Ireland, Scott inherited his vicious hatred for Catholics from the religious tensions of his homeland. Scott immigrated to Canada in about 1863, where he promptly joined the militia. Standing 6'2", Scott was sinewy, strong and almost psychotic. He was always eager to test his talent for brawling and would take on any man at the slightest provocation. Arriving in Red River with the Dawson Road crew, he was fired for assaulting his boss the moment the work gang arrived in Winnipeg. He then took up with Schultz's Orangemen against the Métis.

the fall of "Fort Schultz." Boulton was a staunch British Imperialist and former military man who had little love for anyone who wasn't white, spoke English and loved the Queen. Having supported McDougall the previous year, Boulton had been the first in line at the Old Stone Fort when Colonel Dennis was recruiting men for his fleeting police force. Boulton's sympathies were with the rebels, and even though he was shocked at the sad state of the Canadian force— untrained farmers, many armed with only clubs or pitchforks— Mair and Scott didn't have much trouble convincing the former major to join them.

Boulton probably wouldn't have joined Mair and Scott if the Portage la Prairie party was the only force planning to liberate the prisoners at Fort Garry. But in fact, English-speakers from all over the region flocked to the cause; the bulk of the insurgents were gathering in the English parish of St. Andrew, north of the Hudson's Bay fort. John Christian Schultz didn't waste any time after he recovered from his escape in Robert MacBeth's home. Leaving his reluctant host as soon as he could walk, Schultz headed north to St. Andrew and began rallying men to his cause with an evangelical zeal, and when the day for action arrived, he had mustered together a force of 300. Schultz also sent word to his Métis crony, William Dease, instructing him to start forming a group of anti-Riel Métis to strike the southern parishes in Red River. Schultz was hoping that the garrison at Fort Garry could divert enough men to Dease's uprising and that the combined forces of Schultz, Mair and Scott would be able to overwhelm the remaining defenses.

On February 10, the same day that Riel had successfully completed the treacherous navigation to a provisional government, Mair, Scott, Boulton and company arrived in Headingly, about 15 miles west of Winnipeg. A fierce snowstorm had just begun to gather, and the contingent was held up by the weather for two days. They managed to recruit 40 more men while they waited.

Rumors had begun to filter into Fort Garry by this time. Two English representatives who had participated in the convention

A group of armed Métis scouts, skilled marksmen who knew the land intimately and some of the deadliest fighters on the prairies

debates, Kenneth Mackenzie and F.T. Lonsdale, left Fort Garry to investigate. They met up with Boulton's force in Headingly on February 12, but their attempts to talk the rebels out of going any farther turned out to be nearly lethal.

"You are traitors, pigs and cowards!" roared Thomas Scott, who was on one of his usual drunken binges.

"You don't understand," Lonsdale said to Boulton and Mair while looking nervously at the enraged Scott. "The provisional government is planning to release the captives at Fort Garry any day. We're just waiting for Riel's word."

"You dog!" Scott spat at Lonsdale's face. "How can you stand there and say that you're waiting on the word of a stinking Métis animal? Were you born a groveling mongrel? Or did your Métis masters teach you to be that way?"

Lonsdale tried to get in another word but quickly clammed up when the drunken Scott pulled his revolver.

"What was that?" the soused man slurred, glaring through bloodshot eyes. "Were you saying something?"

Things might have taken a deadly turn at that instant if Boulton and Mair hadn't restrained Scott. The two delegates promptly deduced that their mission was hopeless and headed back to Fort Garry, leaving the shrieking Scott behind them.

At the same time, a Métis patrol intercepted two Half-breed messengers who were carrying orders from Schultz to Dease regarding the upcoming attack on Fort Garry. When Riel got the news, he ordered a full mobilization of his Métis volunteers, and by the next day, over 500 armed men were gathered in Fort Garry. The authorities wasted no time in going after the traitor in their midst, but Dease just barely escaped capture, slipping out the back window of his house and onto his horse as Métis soldiers burst through the front door.

Ironically, all of this occurred on February 12, the same day that Louis Riel decided to start setting the Canadian prisoners free. He had made up his mind the day before, and by first light on the 12th, the captives in Fort Garry were told they could go if they signed an oath not to take up arms against the provisional government. Many of the prisoners were anxious to get out of the fort and signed their names as soon as the document came their way. Others, however, hesitated, mistaking the oath of non-violence for a pledge of allegiance. Riel even went through the trouble of having Andrew Bannatyne explain the oath to those wary prisoners who were unable to read. One by one, the men agreed to the terms, and 16 of the 30 prisoners had been turned loose when word of the imminent attack reached the fort. The remaining 14 men could only watch in dismay as the doors that had been opened to them earlier that day were locked and barred once again, courtesy of Schultz and the rest of their advancing "liberators."

Fort Garry was buzzing with hundreds of angry Métis riders who were spoiling for a fight. Louis Riel was pacing in his fort headquarters, trying to ignore the hubbub of the men gathered outside, when Ambroise Lépine, commander of the Métis force, stormed into the room.

"There are hundreds of men out there, Louis; they've come from all the parishes," the grim buffalo hunter said. "Each of them, to a man, wants to ride out and thrash these fools. Just give the order, and it will be done."

Riel stopped his pacing and looked for a long moment at the flushed face of Ambroise Lépine. Looking out the window into the courtyard, he saw an army of angry Métis with similar expressions. Bulked up in their enormous buffalo-skin coats and bristling with rifles, shotguns and revolvers, the gathered fighters were a fearsome sight, and Riel felt a sudden surge of pity for the men who would stand against them. Riel knew that both Schultz in the north and Mair to the east were poorly equipped and would be slaughtered by the Métis force before him.

"I cannot give the order, Ambroise."

The buffalo hunter looked like he had been slapped. "But why?"

"You know as well as I that those poor Canadian fools would be eaten alive by the men outside."

"With all respect, Louis, I think that is the point. They have gathered an army to attack us. They have even recruited from our old enemies, the Salteaux and the Sioux. These men want us dead, and I, for one, have no problem returning the sentiment."

"Nor do any of the men outside," Riel noted. "But Ambroise, if you ride out and massacre *les anglais*, any chance at moderation in this community, all the work we've done to unify this region under our provisional government, will be for nothing. There would be no peaceful negotiation with Canada; we would be turning our guns against ourselves." Riel walked up to Ambroise and put a hand on the big man's shoulder. "Let's wait before we do anything too rash."

Riel went to work, sending out two conciliatory letters to William Dease.

"Please, William," Riel wrote, "do not sunder the Métis community any more. There is still a place for you here, if only you accept the provisional government."

Riel then met with John Sutherland, a well-established Scottish settler from Kildonan, who was just as concerned with the direction things were taking as Louis was. After learning that Schultz's 300 men were marching south from St. Andrews to Kildonan, he rode to Fort Garry to tell Riel, hoping that diplomacy might turn the rising tide of violence. Louis certainly entertained the same hopes.

"I implore you, Monsieur Riel, do not send your army out after John Schultz," the Scot said. "For I do not believe the English in Red River will follow you after such a massacre. Indeed, such an action might throw the region into civil war."

"You are right, Mr. Sutherland," Riel responded, "I'm fully aware of the gravity of the situation. But what would you have me do? There are armed men approaching my community. Am I to tell my people not to defend themselves?"

Sutherland thought carefully before he replied. "Word is that they are coming to free the prisoners in this fort. I hear that you've already freed most of the men who stood against you last year. What if you free the rest?" Sutherland looked carefully at the Red River president. "Such an action would deprive Schultz of his reason to attack and prove that you are a moderate man."

"Or a weak man," Riel replied.

"Please, Monsieur Riel. What difference would a handful of extra Canadians make to the hundreds that are gathering? If you set those men free, I will carry the good news to Kildonan and use all my influence to convince Schultz to put down his weapons."

Riel sat in silence, mulling over what Sutherland had just said. The Scot's words had gotten through to him. "I will consider what you have told me today, Mr. Sutherland, and give you an answer tomorrow."

First thing the next morning, Riel called the Scot to his office. "Eat your breakfast here and then return to your home. Tell everyone in Kildonan that I am going to release the rest of the prisoners."

Sutherland smiled at the Métis president, shook his hand and then dashed out the door. He didn't bother to have his breakfast.

Meanwhile, the Canadian forces were converging on Kildonan. Boulton, Mair, Scott and company approached from the west, and Schultz's army was marching down from the north. Schultz's troops were in particularly high spirits. They had recovered an old, abandoned cannon from the Old Stone Fort, which they were confident would be instrumental in smashing through the walls at Fort Garry. Somehow, the fact that multiple loaded cannons—newer ones, with better range—would be trained on them from the protection of the fort didn't faze them. Nor did the fact that they were planning to attack a force that was better armed, better supplied and larger than theirs. Brimming over with an enthusiasm that was closer to idiocy than heroism, Schultz's men sang a song for the occasion:

> *Hey, Riel, are ye waking yet,*
> *Or are your drums a-beating yet?*
> *If ye're nae waking, we'll nae wait*
> *For we'll take the fort this morning.*

However groundless the men's confidence was, it only increased when they arrived in Kildonan on February 15 to find that Boulton's group was there waiting for them. It was a joyous reunion, and the rebels took heart in their bolstered numbers. Many of the settlers in Kildonan, however, did not share their enthusiasm. Some of the local farmers tried to convince the Canadians that their plan was madness, that they would engulf Red River in a horrific civil war, which they would surely lose. But the leaders of the insurrection would hear no such thing, and a drunken Thomas Scott dismissed anyone who wanted to give up on the attack as a "bloody coward."

Whether such advice was cowardice or common sense may have been uncertain, but the word "bloody" coming out of Scott's mouth sounded disturbingly prophetic. On the same day the two rebel forces united, the Canadians arrested a Métis man named Norbert Parisien. Norbert was a confirmed simpleton. Weak-minded and lame from the day he was born, the unfortunate man had depended on the charity of the community his entire life. Parisien was out walking near Kildonan when he heard the revelry of Schultz's men, and he wandered into the township to see what all the fuss was about. Schultz's men quickly apprehended the poor man because they were convinced that he was a Métis spy.

Terrified and confused, Norbert spent the night locked in a farmhouse. The next day, the frightened Métis was desperate to make his escape. He made his move during a trip to the outhouse, dashing off the moment he was out of sight of the guards. Stopping only to grab a double-barreled shotgun from a nearby sleigh, the frightened man kept running until he reached a stand of trees near the west bank of the Red River. For a moment, Norbert thought that he was clear, and a smile began to creep across his face. That was when he heard the sounds of a galloping rider tearing across the snow towards him. Tragedy was about to strike.

Old John Sutherland had just returned from his meeting with Riel. Galloping to his farmhouse, the exhausted old timer called out to his son. Young Hugh Sutherland emerged from the log cabin.

"Father, are you alright?" he asked.

The tough old Scot shrugged off the question. "Get on your horse. Ride as fast as you can across the river to Major Boulton and Dr. Schultz," he told his son. "Tell them that Louis Riel is setting all the prisoners free! There will be no need for bloodshed."

Hugh Sutherland had inherited his father's temperament and was overjoyed at the news. "Right away, father!"

With these words, the young man ran into the stables and leapt upon his horse. A moment later, he was tearing off the Sutherland farm towards Schultz's camp. It was the sound of Hugh Sutherland's galloping approach that Norbert Parisien heard while hiding along the riverbank. Parisien barely had time to think before Sutherland was right in front of him—not that thinking would have helped. Assuming that Sutherland was coming for him, Parisien raised the stolen shotgun and fired. Hugh was blasted off his horse into the snow, a gaping hole blown through his chest.

Parisien's captors came running when they heard the gun blast. They found a befuddled Norbert Parisien standing mutely over Sutherland's bleeding body, unable to comprehend what he had just done. Sutherland was still alive, barely, clinging to life with each gurgling breath.

"Jesus!" one of the men yelled. "It's John Sutherland's boy, Hugh!"

"That bloody savage shot Hugh!" another man yelled.

Norbert was still lost in his shocked trance and barely heard the men as they approached. They picked up the wheezing youth from the blood-soaked snow and rushed him to Dr. Schultz. The rest of the men exacted their revenge on Norbert Parisien, led by none other than Thomas Scott, who did his work on the poor man with sadistic glee.

"Look what we have here," Scott leered at Norbert as he trudged through the knee-deep snow. "A murdering Métis bastard too stupid to run." Scott stood right in front of Norbert. "Did you forget how?" Norbert didn't make a sound. "Stupid bastard," Scott muttered just before he struck Parisien across the head with the back of his hatchet. Norbert went down instantly, but Scott didn't stop there. Seized by a sudden bloodlust, Scott kept at Norbert's unconscious form, bringing his hatchet down over and over again as he screeched a series of obscene epithets at the man who could no longer hear. The scene got so bloody that Scott's companions finally had to drag him off the prostrate Parisien. Even then, Scott kept screaming his manic anger at the mangled mess that was once Norbert Parisien.

Hugh Sutherland died the following morning, though not before he made a last-ditch effort to salvage his mission of peace.

"Please don't take any revenge," he managed to say with his final painful breaths. "The poor simple fellow was too frightened to know what he was doing."

Sutherland could not know that revenge had already been taken. Somehow, Parisien managed to hold onto life for more than a month before succumbing to his horrendous injuries. He never regained consciousness from the beating that Scott delivered on him and died without a word.

The two deaths bound the frozen prairie with a bristling tension. Rumors flitted about like mayflies. Some said Schultz's force was growing by the day, and he was ready to assault Fort Garry at any time. The Métis waited, almost impatiently, for what they believed was an impending attack. The fort was near bursting with arms and ammunition, and every man in Red River slept with his revolver under his pillow. Winnipeg shops were closed. Women and children were evacuated. One of Louis Riel's captains, William O'Donoghue, led a group of Métis soldiers to scour the town for weapons and ammunition. Bannatyne made the mistake of refusing to surrender the keys to his magazine, and O'Donoghue promptly had it torn apart. By the time the Métis rode out, there wasn't a single keg of gunpowder left in Bannatyne's store. Events were inching ever closer to war.

Amid the tension, a man named Norquay came to Fort Garry to report that the English parishes would no longer support the provisional government. Riel, sensing that the Red River was about to dissolve into chaos, desperately sent a quick, impassioned plea back with Norquay to the armed Canadians at Kildonan. It read:

> *Fellow Countrymen,*
>
> *Mr. Norquay came this morning with a message, and even though he has been delayed, he will reach you in time enough to tell you that for my part I understand that war, horrible civil war, is the destruction of this country. And Schultz will laugh at us all if after all he escapes. We are ready to meet any party. But peace and our British rights we want before all. Gentlemen, the prisoners are out, they have sworn to keep peace. We have taken responsibility for our past acts. Mr. William Mctavish has asked you for the sake of God to form and complete the provisional government. Your representatives have joined us on that ground. Who will now come and destroy the Red River Settlement?*
>
> *I am your humble,*
> *poor, fair & confident*
> *public servant*
> *L. Riel*

The message reached the rebellious lot in the wake of the tragic death of Hugh Sutherland. Since Sutherland's murder, something was happening in Kildonan. It was as if every fighting man gathered under Schultz saw their own potential demise in Sutherland's purposeless death and decided that war might not be such a glorious thing after all. It did not help that the women of Kildonan, heartbroken at the loss of the fine young man, raised a voluble fuss over the futility of Schultz's uprising, sufficiently deflating any perceived gallantry from the movement. On top of these pressures, Louis' conciliatory letter suddenly deprived the men gathered at Kildonan of their primary antagonist, and it wasn't long before Schultz's force began to dissolve. The nearly 400 men began to drift away, and by February 18, there was next to no one left—even Charlie Mair had deserted the cause. Predictably, the uprising ended with more than a little bickering. The still-ardent Scott bandied the word "coward" about like a stick. Sadly, it worked with a small minority of about 50 men, who decided on a foolishly provocative show of bravado. Hoping to make a statement of defiance, these remaining Canadians planned to march right past the Métis, who were still armed to the teeth and anxiously holed up in Fort Garry.

A show of strength or a show of stupidity? Boulton must have believed that the maneuver fell into the former category, for along with Thomas Scott, he agreed to lead the foolhardy 50 on their pointless mission. To his credit, he did at least order his men that, on no account, were they to open fire on the fort—an order that applied only to those troops who had guns to shoot. Even so, Boulton had enough military experience to know that if only one of his men opened fire on the Métis, their little show could turn into a massacre.

As it was, the marchers were already treading on thin ice. One of the 50, a man named William Sanderson, would later write: "Riel had sent word that we should follow the road, and if we had any arms, we should keep them to ourselves and not make any show of them. There is no doubt everything would have been all right had we followed the road as we were bid."

Instead, Boulton deliberately ordered the group to head off the road and march straight in front of the fort. Actually, "marching" is too dignified a word for what these Canadians did in front of Fort Garry. For as soon as they stepped off the road, they found themselves thigh-deep in snow, and despite the defiant little column's determination to maintain a martial appearance, they found that it was all they could do to inch forward, one struggling step at a time. If there was ever a time when Boulton's military pride was damaged beyond repair, this sad march would have been it.

From atop the towers of Fort Garry, the Métis watched in mounting alarm as the group of men veered off the road. What were

the Canadians doing? Was this some sort of ruse? Where was the rest
of the force? Were they trying to surround the fort? Clearly, the
Canadian intentions must be hostile to so blatantly ignore Riel's
directions. As the Canadians got closer, a group of Métis cavalry
burst out of the fort and plunged through the snowdrifts to intercept the small contingent of struggling men.

Everyone in town crowded for vantage points as the Métis
hunters bore down on Boulton, Scott and their hapless followers.
Every window was packed with faces; young boys were precariously
perched on fence posts; and there wasn't a single woodpile that was
not capped by eager spectators cheering on the horsemen. Perhaps
the more compassionate among the Métis uttered a silent prayer
for the souls of *les anglais* who were floundering in the snow, but
most of those looking on were probably thinking more along the
lines of carnage. At least it can be said that the Canadians were not
foolish enough to grant the Métis spectators their wish. Surrounded,
outnumbered and outgunned, they surrendered without much fuss,
and a mere two days after the jail cells were emptied, they were filled
with cursing Canadians once again.

By now clemency was beginning to look like an ineffective strategy to Louis Riel. The patience of his military council was used up. It
seemed as if Schultz's faction translated the provisional government's lenience as weakness. Perhaps it was time to make clear how
serious the Métis actually were. This was no game. These Canadians
and their sympathizers had been in open and armed rebellion
against a legitimately and democratically formed government. Their
belligerence and irresponsibility had precipitated two murders and
had come within a hairsbreadth of far greater evil. To Métis eyes it
had clearly been treason, and a tribunal sentenced five perceived
ringleaders among the captured lot—Boulton and Scott among
them—to be executed.

Still, the harsh, though hardly undeserved, judgment conjured
cries for mercy. One of the most moving came from the mother
of the recently slain Hugh Sutherland. The Sutherlands were

Riel, the young leader of the Métis, during the Red River Resistance, from 1869 to 1870

prominent settlers in the region and knew the Riels quite well. Mrs. Sutherland spoke privately with the young Métis president whom she had known as a quiet little boy not so many years ago.

"There's been too much bloodshed already," she pleaded with moving magnanimity. "There must not be any more."

With difficulty, Riel stood firm. "They must pay for their crimes," he replied simply.

More entreaties flowed through his doors, however, and Riel was eventually moved to relent. He ended up commuting all of the death sentences, save the sentence for Boulton. The former major was the proclaimed leader of the rebel army, and Riel was determined that he be held responsible. Nevertheless, his sentence was reprieved until the next day.

Many more English-speakers came to plead, but Riel kept his mercy under lock and key just as he did the prisoners. Until, that is, a visit by Donald Smith on the morning of February 19. It should be noted that the only account of this fateful conversation is courtesy of Smith's later report on the events. Still, it seems that the Montréal busineeman argued his case convincingly. Smith warned his Métis adversary that Boulton's execution threatened to divide the settlement that Riel had struggled so hard to unite. Of course, Smith was right, and Riel knew it.

"As always, Mr. Smith, you are persuasive," Riel said, a small smile playing across his face. "Until now, I've been deaf to all entreaties, but your words of reason have reached me. I will consider granting this man his life. But in so doing, I must ask you a favor."

"Anything that in honor I can do," Smith replied, "I shall."

Riel hated the discord that had spread its poisonous tentacles through the settlement and undermined his provisional government. He now saw an opportunity to transform the considerable opposition of Donald Smith into a tool for his cause.

"Will you use your influence to reunite us?" Riel asked his erstwhile opponent. "You can do so and perhaps prevent the bloody claws of civil war that threaten to grasp this entire region."

Smith thought carefully before he replied. "Like you, Monsieur Riel, I am a peace-loving man. If you spare Boulton's life, I will do all I can to see that the English participate in the provisional government."

"If you can accomplish such a thing, you will have averted a war in Red River," Riel replied. "And in so doing, you would be responsible for saving far more than the life of a single crackpot ex-major—on your success depends the lives of all who live in Red River."

By February 26, Smith's efforts had been successful; the English parishes were back on board with the provisional government. Again, success had been pried from the jaws of disaster. Smith always proudly maintained that he had managed to persuade Riel to spare Boulton's life, which could very well be true. But others have speculated that Smith had actually played right into Riel's hands, that Riel had no intention of executing Boulton at all and had just used the threat of the execution to lure the influential Donald Smith to his side. It cannot be denied that the move made Riel's longtime adversary into a bolstering pillar for his cause.

In any case, with the hopes for a provisional government again on firmer ground, Riel finally succumbed to the crushing pressures of the previous few weeks. On February 24, he came down with an illness. A foreboding omen of the sort of health difficulties Riel would suffer in the future, the sickness was called a "brain fever" by more than one doctor who examined him. But under the tireless care of his family and the Grey Nuns, Louis was soon ministered back to health. He would be fine—for now.

CHAPTER FIVE

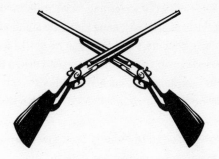

Execution

MOST OF THE CANADIAN REBELS who had put on their ludicrous show of defiance in front of Fort Garry accepted their incarceration with surprising humility and good grace. For their part, the Métis made it as easy on them as they could, treating the Canadians with careful respect, making sure that each of the prisoners received the same rations as the Métis soldiers. Within a few days, a strange and surprising accord developed between captors and their captives, and it wasn't unusual to see the Canadian prisoners sharing laughter and coffee with the guards. It was one of the ironies of the Red River uprising that some of the staunchest Canadian rebels were able to develop civil relationships with their captors during this time. Perhaps several Canadians even began to question their own animosity towards the Métis—those Canadians, that is, who were capable of self-exploration.

Thomas Scott wasn't the sort of man who cultivated civil relationships with anyone, French or English, but he saved the worst of his acerbic nature for the Métis. In an epic display of pig-headed bigotry unparalleled by a single man in Canadian history, Scott did everything he could to make every moment of every day unbearable for his guards and his cellmates. From morning until night, Scott stood at the door to his cell screeching racial insults at those on the other side of the bars, scarcely giving himself a moment to breathe between the string of curses and slurs that he hurled without end. Métis guards and Canadian prisoners were soon driven beyond irritation by Scott's constant high-pitched invective.

"*Mange le merde, enfant de chien!*" Métis yelled at the deliriously angry Scott.

"For the love of God and the Queen, Scott, give that mouth a rest!" Canadians cried in exasperation.

But there was no getting to him. In fact, if anything, he seemed to get worse with each passing day, carrying his racist tirades later and later into the night, keeping everyone in the fort from sleep. It got so bad that the soldiers of Boulton's former army, all locked in the same room, pleaded with the guards to have Scott removed from the cell.

"If you don't have an isolated cell to put him in," one of the Canadians said, "then take him out and shoot him. I don't care, just stop the noise." Every time Scott was escorted to the outhouse, he prodded, kicked and scuffled with his guards. No one knew what to do with him.

Then one day, for reasons unknown, another prisoner named Murdoch McLeod decided to join him. On March 1, McLeod and Scott forced the door to their cell open and fell upon their surprised guards. A violent scuffle ensued, during which Scott and McLeod bellowed at their cellmates for aid. None lifted a hand to help, and when the ruckus attracted more Métis, the pair was quickly overpowered. The guards' collective patience had finally reached a breaking point, and they decided that they would exact some quick corporal punishment right then and there. Scott was hauled out into the fort's courtyard, where the Métis promptly commenced to give him a good beating. Things got carried away when one of the buffalo hunters, overwhelmed by his hatred, pulled his revolver, cocked the hammer and put it to the Orangeman's head. Thomas Scott would have probably been killed right there if a member of the provisional government had not appeared.

"Hold!" the elected representative bellowed to the group of buffalo hunters. "Not a single prisoner is to be harmed."

Apparently, this rule applied even to Thomas Scott. The reluctant Métis led him back into the fort, where he was locked up by himself in a smaller cell. But the isolation took none of the fire out of Scott's rage; the Irishman kept up his diatribes. A few days later, a concerned Louis Riel visited the ranting prisoner. He spoke to him through the grate in the door.

"Mr. Scott, you are winning quite a reputation for yourself. I congratulate you on your performance. We can hear your speeches on the other side of the fort."

Scott's voice cracked from all the days of constant shouting. "Go to hell, you bloody savage!" the Orangeman screamed at Riel. "You may talk like a smart man, but you're just the same as the rest of them—dumb as a mule."

"And you, Mr. Scott, maybe you would do well to talk like a smart man."

Scott's eyes narrowed as he stared at Riel. "Where are my papers?" the man shrieked.

"Papers?" Riel found the sudden change in topic a little bit funny, and he tried to fight the smile creeping across his face. "I know nothing about papers. What sort of papers did you have?"

"You goddamn son of a bitch," Scott barked back, "I'll have my papers in spite of you."

Riel's reply was concise. "That's no way to talk to a human being, Mr. Scott—a man like you should know better, coming from such a civilized part of the country," Riel said, tongue firmly in cheek. "As for your papers, if any such documents exist, you will get them back before you leave. In the meantime, I suggest that you calm yourself. The guards are at wits' end with your foolishness. They have told me that if the government doesn't execute you, they will do it themselves."

Apparently, Scott's near brush with death on March 1 had little effect on him. He sneered at Riel's warning. "The Métis are a pack of cowards," he said. "They will not dare to shoot me." So Louis Riel walked away from Scott, resigning himself to the fact that talking with the man was futile.

Scott was wrong. On March 3, the Métis decided that something had to be done about Scott's fanatical hatred for Métis authority. A tribunal court-martial was called together to decide what to do about Scott. The Métis representatives could hear Scott's continued string of insults from within their council chamber. While treason was the formal charge against Scott, it was largely understood, though unspoken, that he was also being tried for being insufferably irritating. The tribunal presented considerable evidence against him; it was almost impossible to defend Scott's long-standing, open and violent opposition to the elected provisional government. Riel served no official role in the proceedings, but gave some testimony regarding Scott's rabid recalcitrance and finished by asking the tribunal to show mercy. It is not known whether Scott was allowed to call witnesses or offer a rebuttal, but he was presented before the tribunal to hear its verdict.

The vote went four to two in favor of Scott's execution, and Ambroise Lépine, chairman of the tribunal, ordered that Scott was to face a firing squad at noon the following day. Riel translated the fatal sentence to the incredulous young man who was then promptly led back to his cell in chains. Reeling from the verdict, the dazed Scott refused to believe that the Métis would actually go through with his execution.

"They can't do this," he was heard muttering to himself as he was led back to his cell. "It's murder."

Throughout the night of March 3 and the following morning, many people from the English-speaking community came to Fort Garry to plead for Scott's life. But this time, Riel would not relent.

"I take a life to save lives," he said to each of the supplicants who came into his office.

Donald Smith tried to intercede, as he had done on Boulton's behalf two weeks previous; yet this time, Riel wasn't willing to back down. Louis responded to Smith by rolling off the long list of Scott's crimes in Red River.

"What would *you* do in my place, Mr. Smith?" Louis asked. "This man's hostility and insubordination have gotten so bad that he has half the fort plotting his murder. I need guards watching over the prison guards, lest they take his execution into their own hands."

"Mr. Riel," Donald responded, a grave look in his eye. "The one great merit of your resistance to this date is that it has been nearly bloodless. Everyone is saddened at what happened to Sutherland and Parisien, but we all understand that their deaths were tragic." Smith paused, staring at Louis carefully before continuing in slow, measured tones. "But this man's death, should you execute him, will not be understood that way at all. Please believe me when I say, that no matter how reprehensible Scott is, the Canadians will not forgive you for his execution. The English here and the powers in Ottawa will call it a crime. Do not burden your remarkable achievements with such a perfidious deed. Let Scott live."

Riel's eyes lit up in defiance. "How will we ever be taken seriously if we let such a criminal go unpunished? Our authority is a legitimate one, granted by the peoples of this region, and any man who defies it must pay the penalty. The government has reached its verdict, and I will stand by it. Thomas Scott must die!"

Smith sighed and shook his head before getting up to leave. "Very well, but remember what I have told you today. The Canadians will not forget this."

"Forget?" Riel shouted at Smith's back as he was leaving, "I would rather they not forget this. Maybe now Canada will respect us!"

Thus, the last entreaty for Scott's life ended abruptly, with a weary Donald Smith walking out of Riel's office, his dark warning of the public's reaction to Scott's execution hanging in the air behind him. Louis Riel decided to ignore it, not knowing at that time that Smith may as well have written his warning on the wall. For as impossible as it might have been to believe that the dissolute Thomas Scott was martyr material, his execution would indeed make him into a Canadian hero. And just as Donald Smith predicted, Louis Riel would never shake the phantom of the angry young man.

Just before noon on March 4, Scott was permitted to bid a final goodbye to his fellow prisoners and say a brief prayer with Reverend Young before he was blindfolded and led out to the courtyard.

"This is horrible," sobbed Scott as he stumbled towards his end. "This is cold-blooded murder!" Finally, it seemed, Scott had grasped the gravity of his situation.

Not that the poor man could see it, but he was led out into a beautiful winter day. The clear blue sky stretched from cloudless horizon to horizon as Scott was led to one of the fort's walls and made to kneel in the crisp snow. The blindfolded man didn't make a sound when the men who had led him there turned and walked away. The sound of their footsteps crunching over the snow was one of the last things he heard. No one in the solemn gathered crowd so much as whispered. André Nault let a few moments pass before he nodded at the firing squad. The men raised their rifles to their shoulders. Nault then gave the silent signal, dropping a handkerchief from his upraised left hand and letting it fall down towards to the outstretched palm of his right hand. The moment the cloth landed, the Métis riflemen opened fire.

Scott was knocked back off his knees, lying face-up in the suddenly bloody snow, his chest perforated with bullet holes. But he was still alive. A bone-chilling moan escaped from Scott's throat as he twitched under the brilliant blue sky. François Guillemette quickly strode to where the dying man lay. He drew his pistol and placed it against Scott's head, ending the Irishman's suffering with a single bullet. Riel, who had watched the execution in grim silence, stepped forward and ordered the assembled crowd to disperse. Though he made an effort to look stoic in the eyes of his people, everyone could see the terrified pallor in his face.

Riel had displayed remarkable political sense from the moment the resistance coalesced around him, but the execution of Thomas Scott

Thomas Scott's execution sent tremors of fear and rage into English-speaking Ontario. Scott became a martyr, Riel a fugitive.

would prove to be a profound mistake. He later admitted that Scott was executed with the intention of sending a tough signal to Ottawa in the face of his government's imminent negotiations, while also intimidating Schultz and his cronies into obedience. But he did not take into account the massive public outcry that Scott's death would provoke. Rather than scare the voices of dissent into silence, Scott's corpse provided fuel for Schultz's grievances against Riel's government.

It turned out that Donald Smith's warning was prophetic. Schultz's gang used Scott's death as an example of the sort of "barbarism" the Canadians were being subjected to at the hands of the Métis and quickly spread word of the execution east to Canada. The timing couldn't have been worse. For just as the roaring ripple of outrage began to awaken public opinion in the East, Red River's diplomatic delegation was appointed by the provisional government and sent to Ottawa in the hopes of working out conditions of entry into Confederation.

The provisional government chose three men to make the journey to Ottawa. One of Riel's most trusted associates and advisors during the past months, the staunch and reliable Father Noel-Joseph Ritchot, represented the French Métis. The representative for the English community was the sarcastic and condescending Judge John Black. Alfred H. Scott, a bartender in Winnipeg's O'Lone's Saloon, rounded out the trio as the American representative.

The three negotiators departed for Ottawa on March 22, 1870, leaving the Red River just as an optimistic spring began to temper winter's harsh spell. Theirs was a great responsibility: to communicate Red River's list of propositions and conditions under which the community would willingly enter into the Canadian confederation. Riel informed each that the clauses of the provisional government's List of Rights that had been drafted by English and Métis delegates the previous January were non-negotiable.

"Bear in mind," Riel urged the trio, "you carry with you the full confidence of this people, and it is expected that in the exercise of this liberty, you will do your utmost to secure their rights and privileges."

The three men bore a great responsibility eastward, and they left knowing that nothing less than the future of their community was at stake. But Father Ritchot, Judge Black and Alfred Scott weren't the only ones taking leave of Red River.

Following the ignominious dissolution of their ragtag band of rebels that winter, Charlie Mair and John Schultz had split up and fled. Neither Mair nor Schultz had been foolish enough to parade in front of Fort Garry with Boulton and Scott's retinue. Both were marked men; Schultz, in particular, was painfully aware that there had been an outstanding warrant for him since his escape from jail on January 23.

Their plans for taking Fort Garry, capturing Riel and leading Red River's entry into Canada were put on indefinite hold after their little army dissolved, and Schultz and Mair lit out of the region as quickly as they could. Both men barely survived their harrowing ordeals through the severe prairie winter. Schultz would later say that his escape from Red River was a trip through hell: trudging across the snowy expanse of the frozen prairie, he was forced to contend with constant blizzards and temperatures below −30°C. Indeed, it speaks volumes of the man's toughness that he even survived.

Both made it out of Red River and were eventually reunited on a St. Paul, Minnesota, street corner early that spring. Almost immediately, they began plotting their revenge upon Riel for their humiliating defeat. They had both heard of Scott's execution and instantly recognized that the drunken bigot's death could be turned into devastating ammunition for their cause. All they needed was the gun to fire it, and that was ready at hand. The two quickly telegraphed George T. Denison, an old friend of Charlie Mair's who was also a fellow founding member of the infamous Canada First organization.

As the events of the resistance came to light in the East, an infuriated Denison had been doing all he could to inflame public opinion against Riel and the Métis "rebels." However, none of the provisional government's actions—not the treatment of McDougall nor the imprisonment of "loyal Canadians" like Schultz or Mair—had done much to fan the nearly dead embers of public indignation. Denison and his group of rabble-rousers soon became dismayed that nothing they said or did got through to the largely apathetic public.

Everything changed with Mair's telegram to Denison. When the virulent Orangeman learned that Schultz and Mair had been chased out of Red River and that one of their number, Thomas Scott, had met his end at the hands of a band of "Métis savages," his heart lit up with joy. Like Schultz and Mair, Denison quickly grasped the opportunity that such developments presented for their cause. He and his Canada Firsters quickly got to work, putting together a public reception for the two deposed Canadians and taking every opportunity to denounce the murder of that "gallant soldier for civilization," Thomas Scott. The plan was to foment an anti-Riel public opinion so virulent that the Canadian government would be forced to send an armed expedition to quash Riel's resistance.

Denison and his friend's success at reaching the dark heart of eastern fear and bigotry was phenomenal. In a campaign of virulent propaganda the likes of which Canada has seldom seen, the Canada Firsters whipped Ontario public opinion into a blood-thirsty, anti-Riel frenzy. The *Toronto Daily Telegraph*, a paper owned by fellow Canada First member William A. Foster, printed a celebrated obituary mourning "the murder of the brave young Orange-man." Other papers in Ontario, not about to be left in the dust of such a momentous story, jumped on the bandwagon.

Denison stepped up the rhetoric daily. "Schultz, Mair and the other Canadians," he would thunder to assembled crowds from atop his soapbox, "risked their lives in obedience to a proclamation in the Queen's name, which called upon them to take up arms on her behalf."

Denison would then try to look as many men in the eye as he could, casting a disapproving glance, as if to ask, *Where were you?*

"There were only a few Ontario men in that remote and inaccessible region," he would proclaim, "70 give or take, surrounded by an army of half-savages, besieged until supplies gave out."

His articles in Orange papers read like a romantic story by Sir Walter Scott, and with at least as much fiction.

"Is there any Ontario man who will not hold out a hand of welcome to these men?" Denison demanded. "Any man who hesitates is no true Canadian. I repudiate him as a countryman of mine."

The kettle was brought to a boil. On April 7, a huge crowd in Toronto welcomed Schultz and Mair as heroic patriots. A rally planned for the town hall that evening had to be moved to the open square in front of the building because the crowd of 5000 was simply too large to fit inside. Schultz sank to the occasion.

"The Fenian flag floated above Fort Garry," he regaled his rapt audience. "The rebels held high revelry within its walls, and Canadians lay in dungeons within. Canadians! Imprisoned! In lands that are, by the will of the Queen and the Dominion government, theirs by right."

The giant doctor, towering over the enormous crowd, then roared his accusation at the Métis, freely garnishing his rage with generous doses of imperialism.

"Who are these savages who dare to defy the will of the Queen? For it was from her province, Ontario, that this movement to add Red River to the Dominion began," Schultz bellowed. "It is in Ontario that this expression of intolerance towards barbarism and murder will be voiced; and it is to Ontario that the territory will belong once more. My friends, we need only act!"

His speech was followed by a chaotic, impromptu adoption of a series of resolutions by the crowd, supporting the actions of the Canadians at Red River and demanding decisive measures from the federal government to suppress the so-called revolt. The rally was so popular that the Schultz and Mair act decided to go on tour. "Indignation meetings," as they were called, were then held in towns throughout Orange Ontario.

The pair's exaggerations and showmanship would have been humorous if they weren't so dangerous. Mair compared his prison to the infamous Black Hole of Calcutta. Of what Herculean proportions was Mair's constitution that he managed to survive such a traumatic ordeal, the credulous listener must have wondered. Schultz took to holding a coil of rope while speaking, brandishing it like it was a holy relic.

"This," he announced, "is what was used to bind the wrist of poor murdered Scott, whose only crime was loyalty to his Queen and devotion to his country."

Leaflets and posters flooded through Ontario. "Red River Outrage—A Rope for the Murderer Riel," read one. "Orangemen, Is
Brother Scott Forgotten Already?" implored another.

Sadly enough, this snake oil sold all too well, and before long,
much of Ontario's populace was driven into such a fury that the
Canadian government was forced to dispatch an envoy to intercept
the Red River delegates while they were still on American soil. When
the Canada Firsters found out about the approaching delegates, they
became adamant that their government not recognize them. Some
of the more fanatical Orangemen began bandying about the possibility of ridding the world of the troublesome trio that was
approaching. It got so bad that Macdonald sent out an agent to
inform the delegation that it would serve them best to change their
route into Ottawa, warning them that there was a real possibility
that they might be met by a lynch mob in Toronto.

Denison and company had even descended upon Ottawa with
their demands. The mob was given a chilly reception, however, as
Macdonald and George Étienne Cartier had no taste for the kind of
politics touted by the Canada Firsters. Besides, though their governing coalition depended upon votes from Ontario, they also relied
heavily on Québec, whose citizens were likely to be offended by too
stringent an alliance with the Orange lodges against the Métis.

The Canada Firsters, roused to battle, were not to be denied their
pound of flesh so easily, however, and resorted to hiring lawyers who
would charge Alfred Scott and Father Ritchot for "aiding and abet-
ting" the murder of Thomas Scott.

This was the environment into which Ritchot, Black and Scott
were received in Ottawa in early April. One day after he had completed his arduous journey, a disgusted Father Ritchot found that he
had to turn himself in on murder charges. Arguing that he was a representative of the provisional government and ought to have
enjoyed diplomatic immunity, Ritchot was not enthused when the
only assistance Ottawa provided was legal counsel.

Fortunately, the Canada First case was flimsy, and when it came to trial two weeks later, the judge dismissed it in short order for lack of evidence. Ritchot and Scott, priest and bartender, were greeted outside the courthouse by an enthusiastic crowd of supporters with whom Alfred Scott quickly departed on a tour of Ottawa's bars. The verdict did little to lift Ritchot's spirits, however, and he returned to his church lodgings in a foul mood.

The next day, he jumped earnestly into negotiations, eager to get back home as soon as possible. But Macdonald's attitude towards the coming negotiations was clear.

"Once we get them here," the prime minister had commented cockily while they were still en route, "it will be easy to deal with them." Two months earlier he had displayed the same borderline contempt at the idea of Riel coming to negotiate personally. "Everything looks well for a delegation coming to Ottawa, including the redoubtable Riel," he wrote with a touch of sarcasm. "Once we get him here, he is a goner." Macdonald assumed that wily, seasoned politicians of his ilk would have little trouble fleecing the gullible country bumpkins once they had them on their home turf and at their mercy.

Macdonald wasn't far from the truth, as far as two-thirds of the Red River delegates were concerned. Alfred Scott, an American booze-hound in favor of annexation, was a good deal more interested in Ottawa's barrooms than its boardrooms. And Judge Black, opposed to Riel and his aims from the beginning, was more than a little starstruck in the presence of the two political celebrities John A. Macdonald and George-Étienne Cartier; he quickly acquiesced to the Canadians on nearly every single point with a broad grin on his face.

Father Ritchot alone remained true to the trust placed in him by the people of Red River. Ritchot proved to be an unpleasant surprise for the pair of hard-hitting federal politicians. He was stubborn and determined and an effective negotiator. Yet it wasn't until April 25, two weeks after the delegation had arrived, that Ritchot managed to have an actual discussion with his hosts.

The delegates were once more in the midst of another "meeting" disguised all too well as a party. Amidst the drinks and the empty chatter, both of which were flowing far too freely for Father Ritchot's taste, the Métis priest finally put his foot down. Why had the negotiations not started, he publicly demanded of a shocked Cartier? Why had the negotiators not been formally recognized yet? And what of an amnesty for the leaders of the resistance?

"Are we here to talk about the situation of my people or exchange empty pleasantries over wine and scotch?" Ritchot asked angrily in a suddenly quiet room.

It may have been poor manners by Ottawa's upper-crust standards of strained civility, but it worked. On the following day, Ritchot promptly received a letter from Secretary of State for the Provinces Joseph Howe, recognizing the delegation and inviting them to begin formal discussions.

Over the next three days, negotiations began at length and in earnest. Macdonald acceded to nearly all of the pugnacious Ritchot's demands relatively quickly. Yes, "Manitoba"—a name for the region suggested by Riel—might enter Confederation as a province, though Macdonald and Cartier bargained hard to reduce it in size as much as possible.

The main sticking point, predictably, proved to be land. Under the conditions of the 1867 British North America Act, other provinces entering Confederation had retained jurisdiction over their lands. However, Macdonald was unwilling to allow this for Manitoba. To grant Manitoba control over its lands was to compromise Macdonald's dream of a railway opening up the western lands to a flood of white settlers.

Ritchot bargained hard after he realized that land title was a non-negotiable issue. Figures flew back and forth between the humble priest and the powerful politicians until it was eventually agreed that the Métis would be granted title to all lands they currently occupied, plus an additional 1.4 million acres of land for the extinction of their aboriginal title and all the privileges it entailed.

On May 9, 1870, Parliament passed the Manitoba Bill with a land-slide vote, 120–11. The Bill was given Royal Assent—the governor general's stamp of approval—three days later, on May 12. Ritchot must have been pleased as he watched the clauses on bilingualism, denominational control of schools and monies promised to the new province by the federal government become law.

There was one point that disturbed Ritchot greatly, however. Along with many other Catholic priests on the prairies, he worried about his flock in the wake of the likely flood of Protestant Anglo-Saxons that would soon come westward. Ritchot had envisioned a rapid distribution of land to the Métis, enabling them to set up contiguous French Catholic "islands" of land, on which their culture might withstand the coming flood. Ritchot had thought that he had been successful in getting this across—that he, Macdonald and Cartier had reached an understanding on this important issue during the negotiations.

But as the Manitoba Bill moved through Parliament, Ritchot was not at all pleased to see that this point of the arrangement had been altered. There were no provisions ensuring the rapid distribution of Métis lands. Rather, the matter was to be left, in no certain terms, in the hands of the lieutenant-governor. The displeased priest confronted Macdonald right after that session of Parliament.

"The change was only made under pressure from the British Crown, Father," Macdonald consoled Ritchot. "But I assure you, the original spirit in which we negotiated the land distribution will be held up by whichever lieutenant-governor is appointed. In fact, we will make his adherence to your land system a condition of his appointment."

Ritchot chose to take Macdonald at his word and sent a telegraph back to Red River in early May, stating that the Manitoba Bill was, in the main, "satisfactory" and that he was "confident of amicable and acceptable arrangements" to wrap up the negotiated entry into Canada. One might forgive Ritchot for the naiveté of his misplaced faith. After all, Ritchot understood that some compromise was necessary, and given the pressure he was under, the stubborn priest really had stuck to his guns during the negotiations. Rumor had it that just a few days of negotiation with the hardheaded Ritchot had driven Macdonald to his liquor cabinet, leaving Cartier to wrap things up for his impaired partner in politics.

Still, Ritchot's trust would prove misplaced and costly. And the good Father's trust in Ottawa's politicians misled him with one other crucial issue: that of political amnesty for the leaders of the Red River Rebellion. The question of whether legally sanctioned retribution could be pursued against Riel and other figures active in the resistance remained very much an open one. This was one of the first issues that Ritchot had brought up, but Cartier and Macdonald insisted that the Canadian government hadn't formally accepted the transfer of the territory yet, and therefore had no legal jurisdiction in Red River during the resistance. The British government alone, therefore, would have the power to grant amnesty for actions undertaken during the resistance. They further assured Ritchot that such a Royal Proclamation of amnesty was expected from Britain shortly.

Clause 19 of the provisional government's List of Rights demanded an amnesty be granted for all members of the provisional government and those acting under them for all the actions leading up to the negotiations with the Dominion government. If Ritchot was a more suspicious man, he might have insisted upon this point before proceeding any further with negotiations. However, Macdonald and Cartier's explanation seemed perfectly reasonable. Canada, it certainly appeared, did not have jurisdiction in the former empire of the Hudson's Bay Company during the troubles of the winter just passed. Nor was Ritchot negligent in his nagging the government on the promised amnesty from across the Atlantic.

He pressed Cartier with enough verve and persistence that the deputy prime minister once snapped at the priest, "*Mon dieu*. Please Father, I beg you, be quiet about this issue. There is no need to rack your head about this amnesty anymore. You and your people are in good hands. The prime minister and myself know something about this business. You will get your amnesty."

Ritchot even personally contacted the most direct connection to the Queen in Canada, Governor General Sir John Young, who also assured Ritchot that a general amnesty for those involved in the resistance would be forthcoming immediately. Besides, the governor general insisted in a partial contradiction that might have set some alarm bells ringing in Ritchot's head, shouldn't the Royal Proclamation he had issued earlier, which had been presented to the settlement by Donald Smith in December 1869, be enough?

Actually, it was not enough for Ritchot. The proclamation had been dated December 6, and it was only explicitly extended to those who laid down their arms before that date. Would it apply to later events? This was an especially poignant question for Ritchot, given the bloody chain of events that had unfolded in Red River since the date of the proclamation. But in the end, the good Father decided to take the leap of faith and trust amnesty would be granted to participants in the resistance, even though no one in Ottawa granted him a formal pardon. In truth, he didn't have much of a choice, since everywhere he went within the halls of power, all he got were enthusiastic affirmations that amnesty was being looked after.

And so it was that Father Ritchot decided that he had succeeded in his mission and turned his back on Ottawa, leaving the roiling masses of hateful Orangemen behind him to return home—to Manitoba.

Manitoba. He said it to himself and was happy; somehow it sounded like home to him. Little did he know at the time that the assurances for amnesty he had received from the federal politicians amounted to nothing at all. And before long, Louis Riel would be considered an outlaw in the same prairie province that he had fought for and founded.

CHAPTER SIX

Negotiation

IRONICALLY, JUST AS ORANGE ONTARIO had intensified its own social distemper, life in Red River was becoming more harmonious. On March 9, 1870, about two weeks before Ritchot departed for Ottawa, and four days after Scott's execution, Riel addressed his fellow representatives in the provisional government, reminding them of their august achievements.

"Through our own determination and tolerance of each other's differences, we have, for the first time in the history of this land, given its people a voice in the direction of public affairs." Riel was flushed with pride as he made his address, and the representatives responded with cheers and applause. "United as we are, we will make our own terms with Canada."

That was when the representative from Portage la Prairie, that hot seat of English discontent in the settlement, rose to address his community's solidarity with the provisional government. "I would like to tell everyone that Portage La Prairie is in full support of this government, and any rumors that trouble is brewing in my district are utterly without foundation. We are eager to put the disharmony of our past behind us and look forward to discussing our entry into Canadian Confederation with all the people of the Red River."

Magnanimity carried the day, and the residents of Red River seemed to be putting their differences aside in the face of the imminent negotiations with Ottawa. This state of general concord was a great surprise to Red River's old patriarch, Bishop Alexandre-Antonin Taché, when he returned to the community on March 8. Red River's ruling prelate (the same man who had awarded Riel the scholarship for study in Montréal in 1858) had left the region less than a year previous to attend an ecumenical council in Rome. When he departed, the settlement had been in the throes of discord and fear, its people struggling with poverty and divided in allegiance. Taché had only just arrived in Rome when he received a letter from Ottawa informing him of the increased troubles in the community. Returning to Canada with all due haste, Taché had spent much of that February speaking with Macdonald, Cartier and Secretary of State for the Prairies Joseph Howe about developments in Red River.

These talks were Ottawa's first real acknowledgment of Red River's demands and they laid the groundwork for the diplomatic mission that would eventually produce the Manitoba Bill. Though the bishop hadn't been in the region when Louis Riel rose to power, wasn't elected to the provisional government and played no part in the resistance to date, he proved to be an effective negotiator on behalf of his flock. By the time his talks with the Ottawa officials were concluded, he had obtained a promise of amnesty for all those participating in the resistance and laid the groundwork for further negotiations between Ottawa and the members of the provisional government.

Initially, Riel had been suspicious when he heard that Bishop Taché was returning from Ottawa. He knew that the bishop had great influence among the people of Red River and wasn't certain about the motivation of someone who hadn't been anywhere near Red River during the formation of the provisional government but had negotiated on its behalf. Riel knew that Taché was a conservative

Alexandre-Antonin Taché (1823–94), the first Archbishop of St.
Boniface and an influential man in Red River

man by nature, and that he might have been too conciliatory with
the Canadian powers. So it was that Riel treated Taché as another
Canadian commissioner when the bishop returned to the region,
placing him under guard and making sure that he had no contact
with such potential troublemakers as Charlie Nolin. But it became
obvious soon after Taché returned that the bishop was on their side.

Acting as a liaison between Red River and the Canadian government, Taché telegraphed the settlement's Bill of Rights to Ottawa.

In the face of this bolstered Red River authority, the small minority of discontented Canadians opposed to Riel's regime crumbled into scattered and disorganized grumbling. Defeated and leaderless, the most fervent rebels began leaving the settlement. Meanwhile, magnanimity and moderation continued to rule the day in Fort Garry. The English-speaking representatives passed a reconciliatory motion for the benefit of their French counterparts, where they formally upbraided the Crown, the Dominion government and the Hudson's Bay Company for ignoring the rights of the North-west's inhabitants when transferring title of the region. For their part, the French delegates reciprocated by passing a motion that put Canadian settlers' fears at rest regarding the future of the Red River region. This motion was an official expression that the provisional government intended to remain loyal to the British Crown.

Riel was inspired by these developments, and on March 15, ordered the release of the men who had marched on Fort Garry the previous month. Within one week, the jail at Fort Garry was empty once again. A feeling of goodwill seemed to radiate throughout the entire community. It seemed as if a consensus had finally been attained among the North-West's inhabitants, and for the first time in a long time, French-speaking Métis and English-speaking Half-breed dared to look to the future with hope.

There was one bizarre flare-up within the ranks of the provisional government that was sparked by one of Riel's right-hand men, William Bernard O'Donoghue, who had been a trusted member of Louis' government from the beginning. An Irishman and staunch anti-monarchist, O'Donoghue joined Riel's uprising with hopes that the young Métis leader would lead the Red River region away from the British Crown. He had designed the shamrock and *fleur de lis* flag that flew over Fort Garry and had been growing increasingly uneasy as the provisional government cozied up to Ottawa. He wasn't pleased when he learned of Riel's latest order.

As a gesture of goodwill during Ritchot's mission to Ottawa, Riel had the Métis flag at Fort Garry lowered, raising the Union Jack in its place. O'Donoghue was outraged, and behind Riel's back, countermanded the president's order. Now it was Riel's turn to be furious. He ordered the double reversal, with the surprisingly harsh addendum that anyone who tampered with the re-raised Union Jack was to be shot.

O'Donoghue was not put off so easily. Salvaging the old flagpole that had stood over Schultz's former home, he replanted the shaft inside Fort Garry and had the Métis banner raised once again, this time fluttering next to the Union Jack of the mighty British Empire. Riel likely wouldn't have put up with this insubordination if it had been anyone else, but O'Donoghue had proven himself a valuable ally during the past months, and Riel was loath to punish the man for too much loyalty to the Métis cause. He let the flag stand, and for the next few months, a Métis flag and Union Jack billowed together in the prairie wind.

A lighter mood prevailed in the settlements that spring. The good humor wasn't solely owing to the political accord between French and English. Louis Riel had finally succeeded in lifting another burden that had sat heavily on the consciousness of the local population. The Hudson's Bay Company was the hub of the North-West's economic wheel, being the main supplier of goods and money. When the Métis occupied Fort Garry, however, the company had shut down its operations in protest. During the winter, this was no great concern, but as spring approached, the *voyageurs*, hunters, farmers, tripmen and merchants were all desperate to restock their supplies.

On March 28, Riel met with Governor Mactavish, who was still clinging to life, asking him to reopen the company's stores and resume trade. When Mactavish refused, Riel brought up the fact that his people were in dire need of the goods that the Hudson's Bay Company had long supplied in the traditional trading arrangements of the region. Riel posed the problem at his manipulative best.

"You know, Governor, I have only so much control over this region. If the people lose patience, I will not be able to do much to prevent them from simply taking what they need from your stores." Mactavish twitched under Riel's penetrating gaze. "Please remember this if you decide to keep the company's doors locked."

Riel had obviously become accustomed to playing political hardball, and Mactavish found he had little choice but to agree.

"The regular business of the company will now resume without delay," Red River's *New Nation* reported with obvious relief. "This, together with the anticipated lively spring trade, will make good times for all."

On April 8, Riel had grown so confident in the new order of the Red River community that he returned the Fort Garry keys to the Hudson's Bay Company and disbanded most of the Métis military stationed there.

Things were going so well that, on April 7 and 9, Riel issued two proclamations on behalf of the provisional government. Both documents rang with a sense of optimism and triumph. He began by offering a public explanation of why the Métis had felt compelled to deal with Scott so harshly.

"The government, established on justice and reason, will never permit disorder," he explained, "and those who are guilty of it shall not go unpunished. It must not be that a few mischievous individuals should compromise the interests of the whole people."

He called out for the people to put their recent troubles behind them. "People of the North and of the North-West! This message is a message of peace. War has long enough threatened the colony. Long enough have we been in arms to protect the country and restore order, disturbed by evildoers and scoundrels. After the crisis through which we have passed, all feel more than ever that they seek the same interests, that they aspire to the same rights, that they are members of the same family."

"Not only has the provisional government succeeded in restoring order and pacifying the country," he reminded the people, "but it has inaugurated advantageous negotiations with the Canadian government and with the Hudson's Bay Company. You will be duly informed of the results of these negotiations."

And then came Louis' tribute: "People of the North and of the North-West! You have not been strangers, either to the cause for which we have fought or to our affections. Your brethren at Red River, in working out the mission which God assigned them, feel that they are not acting for themselves alone, and that if their position has given them the glory of triumphing, the victory will be valued only in so far as you share their joy and their liberty."

Given what was to occur that coming summer, history would turn his triumphant optimism into sad statements of tragic naiveté. For even as Riel was penning his April proclamations, storm clouds were gathering in the East. The first whispers of coming calamity came on April 19, when Louis received word that a massive Canadian police force was being assembled for the Red River region. He hastily sent a letter off to Ritchot, who was still negotiating in Ottawa, asking about the nature of this force and if it existed at all. Ritchot's response arrived just over a month later. The priest wrote back with a reassuring tone, confirming that a contingent of men had departed for Red River on May 11, but that there was nothing to fear. For as Macdonald had told him, the armed body was sent out solely to pacify possibly recalcitrant Natives, discourage American annexationists whose eyes were fixed north of the 49th parallel and to guarantee Red River residents the impartial protection of British law.

Underneath the prime minister's polished presentation, however, there lay a darker bottom line: the gathering force was being sent out by the Canadian government to impose its will on the upstart region.

As Macdonald had written earlier in the spring, "These impulsive Half-breeds have got spoilt by this rioting and must be kept down by a strong hand until they are swamped by the influx of proper settlers."

Indeed, the only thing that had stopped Macdonald from sending out an expedition earlier was the sheer infeasibility of sending out soldiers across the frozen prairie in winter. But as soon as the spring thaw made the march possible, Macdonald assembled the unit.

The prime minister didn't have to worry about the enthusiasm of the soldiers. A force of 1200 men, the troop consisted of 400 British regulars and 800 Canadian volunteers. The Canadian contingent was brimming with Orangemen whose attitude towards their mission was a deadly mixture of Anglo-Saxon chauvinism and eager belligerence. These Canadian soldiers had wholeheartedly swallowed all the propaganda that Schultz and Denison had fed them. Convinced that the Métis had subjected their Red River countrymen to subjugation, humiliation and horror, these zealous men viewed their march west as a mission of vengeance—for God, the Queen and the British Empire. By all accounts, their commander, Colonel Garnet Wolseley, had no intention of dispelling their fantasies.

Yet whatever air of martial nobility clung to these soldiers as they began their long journey westward was soon dissipated by a rude draft. Their march proved to be excruciating. They were to take the same Dawson Road that Mair and Snow's gang constructed in 1868, but the path had barely been used over the preceding two years and had become overgrown and badly eroded. The expedition suffered through all the classic difficulties 19th-century men associated with the prairies: stifling heat, food shortages, dysentery, mosquitoes and horseflies. They were bogged down in muskeg; their ill-fitting, poor quality equipment was heavy and impractical; and as they slogged through a seemingly endless series of portages, their bones took on a dull and constant ache. All their tribulations had combined to leave the troops in a truly foul mood by the time they neared the newly created province of Manitoba.

Understandably, news of a Canadian military contingent heading their way made the Métis nervous. Father Ritchot, who had returned to Red River on June 17, wrote to Cartier about widespread Métis concerns.

"The setting out of the troops before formal arrangements for amnesty were completed is displeasing to the people. However, I have done my best to assure them of the coming soldiers' peaceful intentions and continue to remind them that your government has promised them amnesty. I am convinced that all will go well, provided that the Queen's amnesty arrives in time."

If Riel began to feel a nagging doubt about the promised amnesty, he continued with preparations for an official reception. He began to work on a speech of welcome to commemorate the arrival of the Canadian force and made arrangements for bonfires, a grand banquet and a special interdenominational church service that all would be able to attend. In a further gesture of goodwill, Riel dispatched four boatloads of Métis to meet the expedition and help them clear the road back from the Winnipeg River. The news the delegation brought back, however, chilled the entire community to the bone. They learned that amnesty was the last thing on the minds of the approaching soldiers. If these men from the East were hungry for revenge when they set out from Toronto, the harsh journey to Manitoba had only sharpened their ire. According to the contingent of Métis who went out to greet them, all the soldiers talked about was revenge.

Suddenly, the illusion that a benevolent Canadian authority had the Métis' best interests at heart was shattered. Until that moment, Riel and so many others had trusted Ottawa's promise that amnesty was on its way. O'Donoghue, Alfred Scott and the Americans in Winnipeg had not been so gullible. With the soldiers' approach, they had persistently nagged Riel that a delegation ought to be sent out to meet the force to demand that an amnesty be produced before they advanced any farther and to threaten that they would be greeted by the sword if amnesty was not granted then and there. It is said that this was when the one and only Gabriel Dumont first contacted Louis Riel. This unparalleled buffalo hunter and legendary warrior who roamed the plains west of the Red River settlement with his

Famed Gabriel Dumont (1837–1906), legendary buffalo hunter and leader of the St. Laurent Métis

own band of Métis sent word to Riel that he could bring 500 men to support such an effort if Riel decided to go through with it.

But Riel postponed his introduction to Gabriel Dumont, opting not to fight the advancing force. Riel was a religious man and abhorred violence. He had put his faith in the Canadian government and the two priests, Father Ritchot and Bishop Taché. Time would show that his faith had been misplaced. Not that the priests were entirely to blame. Officials in Ottawa had assured Ritchot that, while they were powerless to grant amnesty, the Queen could certainly grant a pardon for the players in the resistance. Riel had been content to wait throughout that summer, but Taché grew unsettled when he heard Ritchot's explanation that Ottawa was unable to grant amnesty.

He became aware of a disturbing contradiction in what Macdonald and Cartier had said. In February that year, hadn't the pair promised that their government would grant amnesty to all involved in the resistance? Yet less than two months later, these same men told Ritchot, in no uncertain terms, that Ottawa did not have the power to issue an amnesty for the events that had transpired in Red River that winter—only the British Crown could provide such a pardon. Determined to find out exactly what was going on, Taché traveled back to Ottawa in late June, just after Ritchot returned.

Taché met with Cartier, who was nothing if not reassuring.

"The thing has not changed," the slick politician stressed to the bishop. "We are waiting for a Royal Proclamation every day, and if you remain a few weeks, it will arrive before you leave."

The deputy prime minister even invited the bishop to accompany him on an official trip to meet with the governor general in Niagara. Not nearly as confident as Cartier in the compassion of Britain, Taché accepted.

His meeting with Canada's governor general wasn't pleasant. Sir John Young seemed pained by the presence of the prelate and briskly gave him the brush-off.

"The Queen has already addressed this issue in a previous proclamation. I believe it was delivered to your people by a man named Donald Smith?" Young made it obvious that each word he spoke pained him. "I believe Mr. Smith's documentation covers the whole case."

"But Your Excellency," Taché responded, "the Red River's provisional government has been active since that proclamation. What of their actions since the date of Mr. Smith's proclamation? Will these be covered under the amnesty as well?"

"I don't have any more time talk about Red River, Father," Young gave his dismissive reply. "Talk to Cartier; he knows my views on the matter."

Strangely enough, when Taché returned to Red River on August 23, he maintained to the anxious Red River residents that, while he still possessed nothing concrete, he was sure that the long and oft-promised amnesty was still on its way.

"There is not the slightest danger," he assured everyone.

But by this time, Wolseley's force was practically at their doorstep, and Riel had come to terms with the bitter fact that no amnesty was going to arrive. He took his anger out on his chief negotiator, Father Ritchot, who was also clinging to the idea that the Queen's amnesty would arrive at any moment.

Riel approached the venerable priest in the Fort Garry courtyard on the same day Taché returned from Ottawa.

"Father Ritchot," he began, his eyes staring right through his priest, advisor and friend, "you have failed me." He paused, letting his words sink in. "There is no amnesty coming."

Riel had never spoken to the priest like this before, and Ritchot had trouble concealing the hurt in his face. "Yes it is. Have patience."

"Patience?" Riel exploded. "You ask me to have patience when there are over 1000 bloodthirsty Canadians less than 20 miles away, clamoring for my head? There is no amnesty coming!"

Riel had always been exceedingly respectful of Ritchot, so the priest wasn't sure how to respond.

"But…" he stammered, "they promised me."

"What are promises to such men?" Riel said, his tone softening. "What we needed was a written document." Riel couldn't look at Ritchot any longer. Turning his back on the poor priest, everyone near the pair heard Riel mutter to himself as he strode away. "You have failed me."

What Taché, Ritchot, Riel or even Cartier did not know was that they had all been hoodwinked. The senior French-Canadian politician had honestly believed that an amnesty was forthcoming. He had written a letter to be forwarded to Britain by the governor general, in which he reviewed the recent events at Red River and concluded by recommending a general amnesty for everyone involved. Young did indeed forward the letter, but attached his own statement undermining Cartier's request and stating that Cartier's opinion was only that—his opinion—and wasn't the expression of a united Cabinet. Young hadn't said a word to Cartier or Macdonald about this addition.

Young thus deftly reduced Cartier's request to little more than an expression of personal sentiment. He went even further by including yet another document to the amnesty request, this one a petition circulated by the racist Canada First gang, which opposed any such pardon as "injudicious, impolitic and dangerous." Young made it clear that he personally supported the Canada Firsters, reminding the Crown that Scott had been "led out and butchered in cold blood." So it was thanks to the myopic machinations of Sir John Young that the Queen sided with base opportunists like Schultz and Mair and denied Riel and his provisional government a pardon for their actions during the resistance.

The governor general had out and out lied to Ritchot, Taché and even Cartier, and the three had, in turn, misled the others. While they can hardly be blamed for Young's treachery, Taché, at least, should have been a little more vocal about his doubts concerning the promised pardon. Even on August 23, when Taché returned from Ottawa, and the 1200 vengeful men were a stone's throw away from the fort, he kept his misgivings to himself, somehow finding the gall to reassure Riel that an amnesty was still coming. If Riel had no problem confronting Father Ritchot about his naiveté, he was slightly more deferential to the influential bishop, walking away from him without saying a word.

Riel's situation was desperate. The Canadian army—its less-than-impartial disposition now well-known—was within a day's march of Fort Garry. O'Donoghue had nothing but loathing for the Crown, and the livid Irishman advised Riel that they should either greet the soldiers with loaded guns or not at all.

"We were wrong in trusting any word coming from Crown representatives," he hissed at Riel. "To them, we are nothing but rebels, disturbers of the peace. When the soldiers arrive, they will not think twice about stringing us up by our necks."

There were eager whispers among the Canadian settlers in the area, who suddenly had high hopes for the immediate future. They discussed the possibility of English martial law when Wolseley arrived and speculated over how many of the French would be executed, assuming, of course, that the hateful Louis Riel would be the first to go. By August 23, Riel knew that his provisional government had been caught in a trap, and it was closing around them with fearful speed.

Louis' last night in Fort Garry was not a happy one. The first rumblings of a coming thunderstorm echoed through the prairie night when he called together the representatives from the provisional government in Fort Garry's courtyard.

"My colleagues," he addressed the dour men before him, "as I speak, the Canadian soldiers are approaching, and by all accounts, it does not seem that they are coming in peace. We have yet to hear anything about an amnesty, and I fear the worst for any Métis who is in the fort when they arrive. I advise all of you to gather your belongings and leave the fort at once."

Yet even as the representatives of the disbanded government were hastily evacuating, Riel still dared to entertain a spark of hope. Could the reports of the Canadian soldiers' dark mood be mere rumor? He decided to check for himself. Picking out a few men to go with him, Riel rode out into the pouring rain, hoping that a personal reconnaissance might turn up more promising information. But as soon as they were out in the darkness of the prairie, Riel began to panic. The men that were out with him saw a side of their leader that they had never seen before. He jumped at imaginary sounds in the darkness, whispered anxiously into the night at voices no one else heard and ended up conducting a hushed conversation with himself. It was obvious that the Métis leader was crumbling under the strain of the current events. When they got close enough to see the fires of the Canadian soldiers, Riel was thoroughly spooked and decided that it was best to turn around and head back to the fort.

On returning, Riel changed out of his soaked garb and tried his best to sleep in the near-empty fort, but there would be no rest for the Métis leader that night. He woke the next morning to share a cold breakfast with William O'Donoghue, one of the only other men remaining in the fort. Both were wondering what to do when an English settler named James G. Stewart galloped into the fort and made the decision for them.

"For the love of God, clear out!" the breathless man cried out to O'Donoghue and Riel. "The troops are only two miles from here, and the soldiers speak of nothing but massacring you and your Métis followers."

That decided it. Only when the last glimmer of hope was put out did Riel order the last men to quit Fort Garry. Riel himself rode out of the fort with his stalwart associate, William O'Donoghue, right beside him.

Minutes after they vacated, Wolseley and his columns marched in. Their long-awaited occupation of Fort Garry turned out to be quite a disappointment. There was no boisterous, triumphant welcome, indeed no welcome at all.

"We were greeted by one half-naked Indian who was very drunk," recalled Captain Redvers Buller of their entry into Winnipeg.

The local populace, far from viewing the expedition as liberators were scared stiff about the descent of hundreds of armed and vengeful foreigners upon their tiny community. They remained anxious and behind locked doors.

More disappointing yet, the expedition had been denied the glory of visiting abject defeat on their hated foes.

"It was a sad disappointment to all ranks," Colonel Wolseley recorded in his diary. Worst of all, was the fact that the diabolical Riel was nowhere to be found. "Still," the hateful Wolseley would later write, "at least Riel had not surrendered, for then I would have been deprived the pleasure of having him hanged, as I would have done if I had taken him prisoner in arms against his sovereign." Clearly, Wolseley thought little of Ottawa's promises of amnesty.

Wolseley's troops captured the deserted fort, promptly fired a 21-gun salute, and in proper colonial form, gave three cheers for the Queen. Unbeknownst to them, Riel, O'Donoghue and Ambroise Lépine were watching from a not-too-distant vantage point. It must have been heartbreaking for Riel to watch it all end so. Understandably, he had trouble letting go. He didn't go through histrionics, but was oddly distant, muttering to himself as if he was having difficulty coming to terms with what had just happened. At one point, he even seemed to flirt with capture, moving his horse atop a ridge in plain view of the fort. That was when Lépine and O'Donoghue grabbed the reins of their leader's horse and led him back.

"We must go now, Louis," Lépine said. "We've done all that we can." They crossed the river to St. Boniface, cutting the ferry cable behind them, and stopped in for a brief visit with Bishop Taché.

"You have left the fort?" asked an incredulous Taché.

"Yes, we have fled. It appears that we have been deceived," Riel answered. Taché was still wrestling with his disbelief when Riel became even more blunt. "The soldiers, Your Grace, they would have me and every Métis in the provisional government a prisoner of war. Your amnesty never came. The only thing for me to do is to get on horseback and bolt for the other side of the boundary."

Somehow, Riel managed to remain civil with Taché, even though hot resentment boiled within him. He perceived Taché's fumble as nothing less than a betrayal. In the future Bishop Taché would come to understand that he had been duped. He regretted it deeply.

"I assure you that I am deeply afflicted," he later wrote to Cartier. "I have spared neither pains nor fatigue, nor expense, nor humiliation to reestablish order and peace, and it has come to this, that I am to receive from my own people the cruel reproach that I have shamefully deceived them. It is bad enough to be reviled by one's enemies. I cannot suffer that my people should suspect me of having betrayed them."

Riel likely left with no small measure of bitterness at how badly things ended. But even then, on the same morning Wolseley's men marched into Red River, he managed to find the silver lining. As he left the Bishop's residence with Lépine and O'Donoghue, he fixed his gaze one last time on the scene at Fort Garry.

"No matter what happens to us now, at least the rights of the Métis are assured by the Manitoba Act," he said to no one in particular. "That, in the end, is what I was fighting for. My mission is finished."

Indeed, the scope of Riel's accomplishments had been incredible. In the two years since he had returned to Red River, he had united the Métis against a virulent foe, formed a functioning provisional government and laid out the blueprint for the formation of the province of Manitoba—great achievements. He could hardly be blamed for thinking that his work was done. Little did he know at the time how wrong he was, that for him and the Métis, the trials had only just begun.

CHAPTER SEVEN

Bad Faith

RIEL WAS STRUGGLING with conflicting emotions as he fled from Red River in the summer of 1870. The bitterness at the broken promise of amnesty was balanced by a euphoric sense of accomplishment. As angry as Riel was at the duplicity of the authorities in the East, he was also amazed at the gains his leadership in Red River had yielded. For while the soldiers marching into Fort Garry might be able to send him running, no number of guns could reverse the passing of the Manitoba Bill. The province was here to stay, and the bold, young Louis Riel knew that he was largely responsible for it. But if Louis ever entertained the idea that his work was done in the region, he was sorely mistaken. Indeed, while the triumphs and defeats of the previous year and a half gave Louis a valuable political education, the real schooling occurred over the next five years when Riel learned the cost of dissent. A hunted man from the moment General Wolseley's troops marched into Fort Garry, Riel would not learn this lesson easily.

He left Red River with two of the provisional government's senior members, Ambroise Lépine and William O'Donoghue. From that day on, Louis was able to spend only short periods of time at

home in Red River. And most of these visits were quiet and clan-
destine, conducted with mortal fear as a close companion. The
arrival of the Canadian soldiers in Manitoba ushered in a new era,
and the region that was once Louis Riel's spiritual and physical
haven became a dangerous place for him. If a soldier or the wrong
Canadian settler caught sight of him, Riel's fate could be dangling
on the end of a rope as quickly as a man could say "Treason."

Wolseley's military occupation of Red River was a study in injustice, incompetence and contradiction. On July 22, 1870, when his
force was still approaching Manitoba, Wolseley wrote an official
proclamation to the provisional government. It read: "The force
which I have the honor of commanding will enter your province representing no party, either in religion or politics, and will afford equal
protection to the lives and property of all races and of all creeds.
Strictest order and discipline will be maintained and private property
will be carefully respected." It certainly sounded fair, and given the
cooperation Riel's delegates had received from Ottawa, there was no
reason for any of the Métis to doubt Wolseley's words. Riel had even
personally supervised the printing of the proclamation and distributed it around the settlements to soothe an anxious people.

The very same day that Wolseley's men occupied Fort Garry,
however, it quickly became clear that the colonel's words were about
as reliable as the prairie weather. On paper, Wolseley was willing to
back the doctrine of tolerant liberalism espoused by Cartier and
Macdonald, but in his heart of hearts, he was a soldier, and more
than anything else, he was itching for a fight. After the long and difficult march to Manitoba, he was practically heartbroken that no
fight presented itself in Fort Garry.

Later, when recalling the incident, Wolseley wrote, "I had looked
forward to advancing on the fort in all the pride, pomp and circumstance of war." When it became obvious that there was no need
for such "pride, pomp and circumstance" Wolseley promptly made
an enemy of the Métis, as if to justify his own presence there. Proper
administration of the community was the last thing on his mind.

Referring to the Métis as "the banditti who recently oppressed Her Majesty's loyal subjects in Red River," Wolseley more or less let his men run amok.

The soldiers' conduct in Red River was appalling. Most of the Canadian recruits were Orangemen who had joined the expedition for the sole purpose of exacting a misguided vengeance on the people who had murdered the now-mythical Thomas Scott. Before they left Ontario, many boasted that they would shoot any and every Métis who had anything to do with Scott's demise. Their brutal march west had done nothing but stoke their smoldering lust for revenge.

Thus, finding Fort Garry abandoned was, in Wolseley's words, "a sad disappointment to the soldiers," who were expecting fire and bloodshed at trail's end. But when they got to the fort, the only signs of life were one drunken Native stumbling through the courtyard and a plate of Louis Riel's half-eaten breakfast. Enraged, some of the troops began smashing and looting the fort until Wolseley reminded them that they weren't sacking "rebel" lucre but Hudson's Bay Company property.

They took their anger elsewhere. The troop headed to the watering holes in Winnipeg and promptly availed themselves of every alcoholic beverage they could find. The sparsely populated town was suddenly filled with roaring drunks who remembered nothing of their former duties except that they had something to do with violence. Brawls broke out all over the Manitoba town. Private fought corporal, corporal fought sergeant and sergeant kicked the tar out of private in turn. Any Half-breed or Métis who made eye contact too long found himself pulled into the whirlpool of violence. The drinking binge lasted three straight days, ending only when every saloon in town had been drunk dry.

At the request of Colonel Wolseley, Donald Smith served as interim lieutenant-governor during the military occupation, but the Hudson's Bay businessman did next to nothing to curb the chaos. He limited his legislation to putting out a warrant for the arrest of Louis Riel, Ambroise Lépine and William O'Donoghue and ordering

Adams G. Archibald (1814–92), first lieutenant-governor of Manitoba and the North-West Territories

the bars be shut down at night. Stunned by the soldiers' madness, Manitoba residents put their hopes in the new lieutenant-governor. The word was that Adams G. Archibald was an upstanding man, fair and liberal-minded, free of the virulent racism that the Canadian soldiers swamping the streets of Winnipeg wore like a badge. Archibald arrived just over a week after Wolseley's men, but whatever hopes Manitobans had for the lieutenant-governor's arrival would soon be dashed. To his credit, Archibald did try to institute a fair, civil government; his authority, however, was undermined by another group of subversives that set up shortly after him.

On September 18, 1870, Loyal Orange Lodge No. 1307 was established in Winnipeg. The racist organization saw hundreds of new recruits that month, as many Canadians settlers arriving in the wake of the army joined disbanded soldiers who decided to settle in Manitoba. Lieutenant-Governor Archibald was concerned about the attitude of these new residents.

"There is such a frightful spirit of bigotry among a small but noisy section of our people," the lieutenant-governor wrote the prime minister, "who really talk and seem to feel as if the French Half-breeds should be wiped off the face of the globe."

Schultz and Mair, gleefully triumphant, were numbered among the returning Canadians, and the pair marched back into Red River as if they were conquering heroes.

"We are now in a position to revive the *Nor'Wester* and to print any moral sentiments we please," Schultz wrote to his ally George Denison. By this time in his career, Schultz had mastered the art of printed propaganda, and with his old newspaper back in his hands, the angry Canadian rabble was putty in his hands. In no time at all, Schultz rose to prominence in Red River again.

Wolseley turned a blind eye as Schultz and his loyal Canadians carved out their pound of flesh. Homes were ransacked, Métis women were forced to strip and dance for the entertainment of these louts, and there were harrowing reports of rape in keeping with the vows they had made back East. Theft and violence descended upon Red River like a plague. The Métis, paralyzed by such deliberate and zealous malice, gave no response—until, that is, dead bodies began to show up.

Elzéar Goulet was a well-liked Métis who had been a member of the tribunal that presided over Thomas Scott's execution. It was a sunny mid-September day, and Goulet was on his way to pick up some mail in Winnipeg when he ran into a group of Schultz's supporters. These Canadians recognized Goulet and instantly took after him. The murderous chase led the lone Métis man and the pursuing throng to the banks of the Red River. Goulet dove into the water and swam frantically for the opposite bank. When the angry mob reached the river, they wasted no time in lobbing a barrage of rocks at the Métis man. One of the stones found its target, striking Goulet in the back of the head and knocking him out. A cheer went up when his body went limp. Unconscious and face down in the water, Goulet was pulled ashore several miles downstream, drowned.

Schultz's boys didn't stop there. Four more dead bodies turned up over the next few weeks, each victims of over-enthused Orangemen eager to run the former inhabitants off their lands. It was a brutal display of power, and not a soul in the community had the courage to do anything about it. Not a single arrest was made, and Governor Archibald could only watch, as sympathetic as he was helpless, while Schultz's gang went about its campaign of terror and revenge.

One can only imagine Schultz's joy during his first month back. The tables had turned completely: having been chased out of Red River by the Métis just a few months previous, he now felt completely justified in returning the favor. And while his brazen lack of sympathy for his Métis rivals might seem incredibly callous, Schultz's brutal crimes would have made complete sense to a man of his cultural assumptions, which labeled the Métis inferior before the might of the Anglo-Saxon man. But Schultz was still missing one trophy. Indeed, for all the glory of his triumphant return, there was a gaping absence in Manitoba that was impossible for John Schultz to ignore: Louis Riel. Schultz wanted Louis Riel.

Of course, Riel knew that the Canadians were hunting him, and he fled south of the border with Lépine and O'Donoghue as soon as the Canadian troops arrived. Just days after Donald Smith had signed a warrant for the trio's arrest, the prairie was buzzing with search parties. But the legal authorities were the least of Riel's fears. Almost immediately after the military occupation, Ontario settlers, both sober and drunk, began roaming about the Red River settlements, ropes in hand, looking to enjoy a good lynching party where the Métis leader would be the guest of honor. Nor could that paragon of impartiality, Colonel Wolseley, have been counted upon for any protection. Indeed, he indicated in his diary that he would have been sorely tempted to join in on the fun.

"I should like to hang him from the highest tree in the place," Wolseley wrote of Riel. "I have such a horror of rebels and vermin of his kidney that my treatment of him might not be approved by the civil powers."

Riel, Lépine and O'Donoghue were hiding out in Pointe-à-Michel, a tiny Métis community just south of the American border, when first news of the Red River atrocities reached them. The deposed Métis leader had trouble digesting the information. For Louis, his leadership of the Red River Resistance was a matter of personal pride. He had come to think of himself as nothing less than the embodied will of the Métis people, and it tortured him to hear about the goings-on in Red River when he could not do anything.

He lasted in Pointe-à-Michel for only three weeks. Despite Taché's letters warning him to stay in hiding, Riel snuck back to St. Norbert with Lépine and O'Donoghue. A secret meeting of only the most trusted Métis was held in Father Ritchot's rectory. The 40 assembled representatives decided that the only way they could get attention in Ottawa was to appeal to Parliament's most feared opponent, the United States. A committee hastily drafted a document for President Ulysses Grant in which they detailed the atrocities occurring in the newly formed province. They concluded by asking the Unites States government to conduct a formal inquiry into the crimes that were taking place.

Riel considered the letter nothing more than a political play against the Dominion government. He hoped that when this request was made public, Ottawa would be forced to address the Métis difficulties in the region because of the risk of losing Manitoba to expanding U.S. O'Donoghue, however, had far more ambitious aspirations. He had long been in favor of U.S. annexation of Manitoba, and his argument was strengthened by the Canadians' brutal occupation. He stated vehemently that they should end the letter with a formal plea to be governed by the United States.

"Absolutely not," was Riel's emphatic reply.

"How can you stand by the godforsaken Crown after all of this?" O'Donoghue snapped back, his face starting to redden. "Have you no pride?"

The tension in the room was thick. Almost every man in Father Ritchot's quarters could speak firsthand about some horrible experience at the hands of the Canadians. Anger and desperation wrestled in the hearts of them all.

"It is not a question of pride," Riel said, trying to control his anger. "We have negotiated a satisfactory arrangement with Ottawa. The Manitoba Act provides us with more privileges than we could ever get from the Americans. We just need to force Macdonald's hand into doing something about Schultz and his men."

"You naive fool!" O'Donoghue was yelling now. "Schultz *is* the Canadians! Things will only get worse with time, not better. The Canadians will get bolder as their numbers grow. If we wait, there soon won't be any Métis on the Red River."

O'Donoghue might as well have just told Riel that everything they had fought for over the previous year and a half was for nothing.

"And you think those south of the border will be any better? Look at how your darling American republic treats every Indian tribe it encounters. At least we have a legal document with Ottawa that guarantees us certain privileges. I doubt that the American cowboys even know what a legal document is." O'Donoghue was about to reply when Louis cut him short. "William, you aren't one of us. You never were. The only reason I tolerated your presence is because of all the goddamn complaining I would have to hear if you were excluded. Get out of my sight."

O'Donoghue didn't have to be cued twice. Grabbing the letter to President Grant, he turned and addressed the room before he walked out the door. "I will make sure the president of the United States gets this letter. Surely, he will be able to do more here than the president of the Métis." O'Donoghue didn't know it at the time, but this exchange drew an indelible line between himself and his former Métis friends. The next time he came to Manitoba, he would come as an enemy.

As for Louis Riel, after the meeting concluded on this inauspicious note, he snuck away to his mother's home, spending a few hours with his family before stealing away into the night and creeping back across the border with Ambroise Lépine. The coming winter was hard. With bounty hunters and spies one step behind them, the pair was constantly on the move, going from the city of St. Paul to the small settlement of St. Joseph to the even smaller Métis enclave of Pointe-à-Michel. They discovered that Schultz himself had personally hired men to shadow them, and for a short while after the occupation, every tree, boulder and brush seemed to be watching their movements. It was a terrifying time indeed, and both Lépine and Riel dealt with it by turning in on themselves, silently dwelling over the unfortunate developments.

Inactivity was hard for Lépine. A physical man by nature, the big Métis hunter did his best thinking on the back of a horse with a rifle in his hands. Not used to isolation or introspection, Lépine spent most of his time wondering what he, personally, could have done differently and worrying about the well-being of his family. Louis also worried about his kin, but he rarely spoke to Lépine about it. Like everyone else in his family, Louis was an ardent Catholic, whose unshakable faith had been cultivated during his years of education in Montréal. Now, with nothing but time on his hands, Louis acquired the habit of embarking on long and involved interior dialogues with his Savior. As the minutes dripped by through the winter of 1870–71, Louis slowly began to formulate his own peculiar twist on the Catholic faith, which he would eventually develop into a bizarre faith that would one day dominate his life. For now, these thoughts were only a diversion to distract him from the idle monotony of the day to day.

A flood of correspondence arrived in early November 1870. Métis from three parishes begged him to run as a candidate for Manitoba's first provincial elections. Yet Louis dared not, although he would have undoubtedly won. He knew that he would surely be arrested if he took his seat in the legislature without being granted formal amnesty from the Crown. There was *still* no news from Ottawa; neither Macdonald nor Cartier so much as whispered about the promised amnesty. The political animal in Riel could only pace restlessly in its cage of isolation as Manitoba went through its first provincial elections. No doubt poor Louis spent more than a few days festering over the current state of affairs, in which he was unable to run for office in the province that he had been instrumental in forming.

Louis and Ambroise were still in hiding when the first round of federal elections swept through Manitoba in March 1871. Louis could only sit and watch as Schultz's Orange "Ontario Party" bribed, beat and terrorized its way into winning the votes for 3 out of 4 of the federal seats. John Schultz himself won a seat and secured a $10,000 federal indemnity for the supposed losses he incurred during the Red River Resistance—two more injustices that the Métis had to bear. And Louis sank even further into his profound depression, withdrawing more and more from the outside world as he lost himself in his daily conversations with God.

Meanwhile, his former associate, the fiery William O'Donoghue, was not content to sit and pray while his hated rivals took control of the region. He had reached Washington, D.C., in December 1870, and presented his case to President Grant, pleading that the United States annex the North-West. Grant listened to O'Donoghue's proposal but decided in the end that there was no firm evidence that the majority of the Métis wanted to join with the U.S. Grant's final "no" was hard for O'Donoghue to take, but the redoubtable Irishman didn't give up.

Convinced that the Métis would rise up against the Canadian authority if someone would take the lead, O'Donoghue traveled to New York City where he sought an audience with the infamous Fenian Brotherhood. The Fenians had been conducting unsuccessful raids across the border for years and were wary of supporting O'Donoghue's plan. Eventually, though, they agreed to supply the weapons if O'Donoghue could muster the men. By the spring of 1871, O'Donoghue was making the rounds through Minnesota and the Dakota Territory, trying to talk every Irishman and Métis that came his way into joining his army, which would ride north, strike Crown forces and form the "Republic of Rupert's Land."

He had little luck recruiting men to his cause, yet was determined to carry out his assault nonetheless, sure that the Red River Métis would take up arms with him when they learned of his coming. On October 5, 1871, O'Donoghue looked north over the American border, his gang of 38 horsemen behind him. He gave the order, and the band charged forward, each man somehow trying to convince himself that a republic could be created with fewer than 50 armed men. Louis Riel would make sure that no such thing occurred.

It is ironic that when Louis Riel finally decided to throw his weight into Red River politics, it was on the side of the Canadian government against his former associate. O'Donoghue had made no secret of his intentions to invade Manitoba, and the entire region was buzzing with word of the imminent attack. An extremely worried Lieutenant-Governor Archibald knew how badly the Métis had been mistreated and didn't think it too far out of the realm of possibility that the community would rise up against him. Desperate to obtain Métis support in the face of O'Donoghue's approach, Archibald called Louis out of exile, asking the influential leader to endorse his leadership.

The political animal in Louis Riel came to life when the lieutenant-governor's request reached him. Still a backer of the Manitoba Act, Riel hoped that a display of Métis loyalty might convince the powers in Ottawa to hasten the long-awaited amnesty. And so Riel returned to Red River, intent on securing support for Archibald's government. At a meeting in St. Vital on October 4, Riel made his argument to the assembled Métis.

"By now I'm sure you've all heard about Mr. O'Donoghue's ambitions with the Fenians," Louis began, his speech-making voice instantly finding its tenor after nearly a year of silence. "I implore you, though things have been difficult under the Canadian administration, give Ottawa more time. Nothing the Americans can offer will equal the rights we have won with the Manitoba Act. We need only wait for the proper authority to assert itself in our province, and things will improve."

"But they killed Goulet!" a man shouted from the crowd.

"Yes, they did, and more men as well," Riel responded. "There is no defending the dogs who have committed such crimes against us. But let me remind you, these are not the men whom we will be dealing with when the Crown takes its rightful place in Manitoba. I admit, our foes in this province are intemperate, treacherous and violent, yet let us respond with loyalty, moderation and calm. If you have ever trusted me in the past, trust me now. Do not join Mr. O'Donoghue."

The crowd dispersed in silence, but Riel knew by a single glance into the eyes of his people that he had gotten through. When he came, O'Donoghue would not have any allies in the Métis.

Thus, Riel gave his support to the government that had labeled him an outlaw. All he asked in return was that Canada live up to the letter of the Manitoba Act and that he and Lépine should finally be granted their amnesty. Archibald wasn't averse to granting Riel's request. In fact, the lieutenant-governor had suggested to Father Ritchot that Riel and his followers would be entitled to "most favorable consideration" if they were to support the Canadian administration during its present crisis. The Métis did more than just stay out of the way.

In what was probably the most magnanimous display in the history of the Canadian West, the Métis actually banded together and formed a militia of a few hundred buffalo hunters to stand against O'Donoghue. A grateful Archibald inspected the Métis troops a few days after they had mustered and knew with a glance at the tough riders that the Canadians would not have lasted long if these men had sided with the Fenians. When the lieutenant-governor got to the end of the column, he received their salute and then turned to shake hands with their leaders, the two fugitives, Ambroise Lépine and Louis Riel. Needless to say, O'Donoghue's foray into the Red River region was a complete failure.

Yet the ever-antagonistic media man, Dr. John Schultz, had no qualms about turning this show of loyalty and cooperation into another political powder keg. Publicly condemning Archibald as a traitor for his cooperation with Riel and Lépine, he wrote George Denison, his propagandist counterpart in Ontario, instructing him to inform their fellow Orangemen of Archibald's so-called treachery. Spreading the malice wasn't too difficult. The men of the Orange Order had developed quite a dislike for Manitoba's lieutenant-governor, resentful at his even-handedness with the Métis. Archibald was roasted in the Ontario press for shaking the "bloody hands" of Riel and Lépine.

Orangemen across the country were outraged, and Macdonald, swayed by the force of public opinion in Ontario, publicly admitted that he was embarrassed by Archibald's collusion with Riel and Lépine. In the end, Archibald was given the velvet boot by Ottawa and replaced by Alexander Morris, a man who proved to be far less sympathetic to Riel and his followers. Once again, the Orangemen came out on top in Manitoba.

As the Orangemen rose, Riel was once again cast to the bottom. Hoping that his assistance against the Fenian raiders would at least earn him the privilege of returning to Red River, Louis did not go back into hiding, but tried instead to go back home to St. Vital. Schultz's gang would not let him stay. They came on the night of December 8, 1871, a posse of 15 inebriated goons, bent on the Métis leader's capture. Riel was not home when the men came crashing through his front door, but his mother and sister were. The Riel women could only scream in terror as the Englishmen tore through their home, brandishing their weapons and destroying everything in sight. When it became obvious that Riel wasn't home, they turned on Riel's mother, Julie, yelling that they had a warrant for her son's arrest. When the terrified old woman responded with mute panic, one of the men pulled his revolver, cocked the hammer and pressed the muzzle against her daughter Marie's head.

"Listen here you bloody squaw!" the man screamed at Julie. "Where the hell is your son?" Riel's mother was so frightened that she just stood there shaking, unable to utter a single word.

"Forget it," one of the men finally said. "Damn Métis crone. Do you think she has anything to say that is worth hearing?"

The man with the revolver pressed against Marie's head wasn't quite finished yet.

"Your son will die tonight. I promise it. If we have to tear apart every house in this parish, we will find him."

The men departed, leaving the two Riel women sobbing .

Fortunately, the gun-wielding man turned out to be far too drunk to stick to his words, and Riel, who was visiting in St. Boniface that night, returned home unmolested. But the sight that greeted him when he returned to St. Vital convinced him that he should leave Red River as quickly as possible, for he realized then that he wasn't endangering only himself by remaining in Manitoba, but was also putting his family at risk.

Two months later, in February 1872, Bishop Taché returned from another diplomatic mission to Ottawa, where he had been arguing the amnesty case for Riel and Lépine. The bishop never forgave himself for failing to secure a pardon for the two men, and his standing in Red River had fallen considerably because of it. Determined to see what he could do, he took the trip to Ottawa late in 1871 and sat down once more with George-Étienne Cartier to discuss the fate of the two men. Cartier had been following the events in Manitoba closely and was genuinely remorseful about what was unfolding there. Nevertheless, his hands were bound by political conditions.

"I have to be frank with you, Father," Cartier said to the bishop, "there is very little chance that your friends will get their amnesty any time soon. We face an election in the coming year, and to tell you the truth, our party is not doing well."

"What does that have to do with Riel and Lépine?"

"Well, if the prime minister does grant them amnesty, we can expect to lose many votes in Ontario."

Taché looked darkly at Cartier. "So in the interests of your party, they ought to just sit around and wait until they are captured?"

"Goodness, no," came Cartier's response. "If they are captured, most of the Québecois who are sympathetic to them would likely turn against our party. Your friends would do best to disappear for a while—go into hiding. If Macdonald wins the coming election, only then will we possibly be in a position to grant your men the amnesty that I personally believe they deserve."

Before Taché left, Cartier gave the bishop $1000 to pass on to Louis. "Tell Riel that for now, this is the best the Dominion government can do. We know we are asking for much."

Taché was loath to offer Louis $1000 in exchange for his freedom, but he did it anyway. Reluctant to be bought off for such a pittance, Louis also resigned himself to the fact that it was too dangerous for him to stay in Manitoba. So it was that on February 23, 1872, he and Lépine stole away in the night, heading south once more across the U.S. border.

They left just in time. Edward Blake, the newly elected premier of Ontario, had used his indignation at Thomas Scott's execution as a political issue, and after he won the premiership, offered a $5000 reward for the capture of Riel and Lépine. The pair spent the rest of the winter, all of the coming spring and much of the summer dodging bounty hunters who seemed to always be one step behind. And so Riel lost himself in his inner conversations with the Almighty once again, falling into a bleak depression that lasted until the next election in Manitoba.

As the date for the federal election approached late in the summer of 1872, Riel's political instinct revived, instantly revitalizing the morose man. Métis support from Red River came pouring in with letters requesting that he run as a Member of Parliament. Louis didn't need much urging, and despite the behest of Macdonald and Taché, decided to run for the leadership of the predominantly French Métis riding of Provencher. Riel was poised to win handily, his trips into Provencher triumphant affairs. Flanked by a cordon of armed buffalo hunters for security, he swept through the streets on horseback, leaving in his wake a throng of well-wishers shouting their support for the outlaw candidate. His opponent, an Irish Catholic named Henry J. Clarke, dropped out of the race.

But local popularity and political success in the Canadian system were two entirely different things. Unfortunately, Riel was to be schooled once again in the differences between the two. Louis' difficulties began when disaster struck Macdonald's Tory coalition. In those days, an election didn't take place all in one day; votes were cast on different days throughout the country. In 1872, Québec voted well before Manitoba, so voters in Red River got word of George Cartier's shocking defeat in his Québec riding before they went to the polls. Without his trusted Québec lieutenant at his side, Macdonald's coalition of Québec Bleus and Ontario Conservatives suddenly appeared to be on shaky ground. Macdonald quickly wired Manitoba's lieutenant-governor, half begging and half commanding him to get Cartier elected somewhere in the Red River region.

The lieutenant-governor knew that the only absolutely safe riding in which Cartier could run was Riel's Provencher. Formal negotiations began with the exiled Métis leader. Louis was quick to see the political opportunity in the situation and stated that he would step aside with only one provision, that Cartier do everything in his power to see that the federal government stuck to the provisions of the Manitoba Act. The government had been slow to secure Métis land rights, and of course, there was still the matter of amnesty. Macdonald wired back promptly, promising that Cartier guaranteed he would do his best to "meet the wishes of the parties."

That was all it took for Louis. He gave Cartier his endorsement, and the old Québecois political mogul won Provencher by acclamation. The Métis were jubilant. Fully aware of the political trade-off that had taken place, they dared to regard the coming administration with some measure of hope. Riel and Lépine expressed the expectations of the Métis in the message they wired Cartier: "Your election in our country has been won by acclamation, and we have reason to hope in the success of the cause trusted in your hands."

But in another of the many cruel twists of fate that so liberally adorned Riel's life, just as a light appeared at the end of the tunnel, the walls collapsed. Unbeknownst to the Métis, George Étienne Cartier was overseas in London seeking treatment for a lethal kidney disease. Fighting for his life, Cartier was hardly in any shape to make a political statement about his new constituency and succumbed to the disease less than a year after his election in Red River. The Métis were back to square one.

A by-election was called for the Provencher riding after Cartier passed away in the fall of 1873. The near-spontaneous support for Riel was so fervent that the actual voting process would have been a mere formality. Nevertheless, there were forces in Manitoba that were conspiring against the popular consensus in Provencher.

Schultz and his cronies, still determined to see Riel and Lépine brought to their version of justice, decided to make another run at his capture. They obtained a warrant for his arrest in Winnipeg, and on the night of September 4, had riders storm his St. Vital home. This time, Louis' mother was more composed in the face of the armed men, telling them that her son had heard of their approach and was already gone. It was the truth; Riel had been tipped off about his imminent arrest and quickly made for the shelter of the nearby Vermette woods, where he stayed in hiding for over 45 days. Lépine wasn't so lucky. Arrested in his home, in front of his family, the formidable Lépine chose not to put up a fight. He was thrown into jail that night and soon faced a murder charge in a courtroom where sentiment was stacked against him.

At least Lépine had a roof over his head. In the deepening chill of fall, Riel was forced to hide out in the woods across the river from St. Norbert. His friends came by regularly with food and encouragement. Schultz's brazen action had only strengthened Métis resolve, and more than ever, they were determined to see Louis win his seat in the House of Commons. Louis' good friend, Joseph Dubuc,

compared Louis' ordeal to the story of King David and his hideout
in the cave of Adullam. Joseph might have brought up the allegory
as a light-hearted jest but Louis took it to heart. Adding the Old Testament story to his ever-evolving personal religion, Louis began
drawing a disturbing number of comparisons between himself and
the biblical king. He would eventually give himself the middle name
"David."

Yet even as Riel struggled through isolation and religious delusions
of grandeur, his popularity surged in Provencher. On October 13,
500 armed Métis hunters led him out of the Vermette woods to
a crowded farmer's field in St. Norbert. Then and there, the Métis
appointed their leader, and Louis won his seat by acclamation. A cacophony of cheers filled the air as the gathered men and women of
Provencher voiced their support for their haggard leader. Louis tried
his best to look enthusiastic, but the strain of past weeks was compounded by the weight of the repeated political disappointments over
the years, and his smile of appreciation looked more like a grimace.

Still, the determined young man was not ready to give up the
fight. On October 21 Riel headed eastward to take his seat in Parliament in Ottawa, despite all the forces stacked against him. He
stopped first in Montréal, to gather strength and support from
Québecois luminaries sympathetic to his cause. Years of isolation
and difficulty in the Red River had begun to get to Riel, and the warm
company of a cadre of Montréal intellectuals did wonders for his
troubled soul. Basking in the glow of prominent Québeckers such as
Honoré Mercier and Alphonse Desjardins, Riel slowly regained his
confidence. For a short time, at least, he found refuge from the
tumult and danger that had become so prominent in his life.

A visit to a French-Canadian community in New England was
desperately needed medicine for young Louis. In Keeseville, New
York, he developed a fast friendship with Father Fabien Barnabé.
The priest and his family became like a second family to Louis, and
the first spark of a future love between Riel and Father Barnabé's
pretty sister, Evelina, was likely struck on this first visit.

The respite was brief. When Riel reached Montréal, he was still a man in need of rest, not quite ready to face the challenges of Ottawa and the thrust and parry of a House of Commons awash in turmoil. The Pacific Scandal had just broken upon a shocked nation, and Macdonald was battling both the bottle and the dissolution of his government. On November 5, Macdonald announced the collapse of his Tory coalition, and another federal election was called. Letters and telegrams from Red River and elsewhere flooded into Desjardins' house in Montréal, pleading with the recuperating Métis leader to run again for his seat in Provencher. All it took was a single word from Riel, and the absentee candidate swept his constituency with 195 votes to 68. Alexander Mackenzie's Liberals won the majority of seats in Parliament and formed the next government, but Louis Riel had won his second federal election.

Ever since his first election to the House of Commons, Riel had been a hot rumor buzzing around the capital: would he force things to a head by showing up and trying to represent his people? What would be the result? Even though he was an elected Member of Parliament, Louis was also a wanted man with a hefty price on his head, and every detective and bounty hunter in Ottawa was watching for the large, wavy-haired Métis with the intense eyes. The problem, however, was that almost no one in Ottawa really knew what Riel looked like. The public was buzzing about the anticipated appearance of the MP from Manitoba, but months went by, and Riel's seat was still empty. After Macdonald's government fell apart, Riel decided that it was time to give Ottawa the show it seemed to want so badly.

March 26, 1874, was a cold, blustery day in Ottawa, and Riel drew his coat tightly about his neck as the team of horses pulled his sleigh across the Rideau Canal from Hull to Ottawa. He shivered at the sight of the impressive neo-gothic Parliament buildings rising in the distance and looked to his friends, Adolphe Desjardins and Jean-Baptiste-Romauld Fiset, for support. His heart pounded with anticipation, excitement and fear. At last, the vaunted Métis leader was going to dip his toe into the simmering political waters of Ottawa.

Louis Riel, about 30 years old, in 1873–74 when he was elected to Parliament

He walked into the Parliament building, unrecognized. Wide-eyed, he roamed through the ornate lobbies like any other elected member, neither trying to keep out of the way nor making any effort to join in conversation with other MPs. After lunch, his parliamentary colleague and friend, Fiset, took Louis to the chief clerk's office and simply introduced the famous Métis as a new Member of Parliament who needed to be registered. This was old hat for the chief clerk, Alfred Patrick, who nonchalantly administered the oath of office to which Louis responded: "I do swear that I will be faithful and bear true allegiance to Her Majesty Queen Victoria."

Still unsuspecting, the clerk nudged the register towards Riel for his signature. Only as he turned the register around did he notice the name "Louis Riel" in ink still wet off the nub. An astonished Patrick looked up just in time to see Riel turn and politely bow as he left the office. Young Riel had to fight the urge to wink mischievously at the dumbfounded clerk.

With a speed decidedly unbecoming of any Ottawa official, Patrick ran through the halls to inform the stunned minister of justice of what had just transpired. In all the excitement, all Patrick could recall about Riel's appearance was that he sported "a heavy whisker that was dark, but not exactly black."

The news flashed through Ottawa like lightning. Authorities feared that riots might occur between the French and English, and extra police were called up. Printed likenesses of Riel circulated through town faster than coin. Private detectives, their eyes hawkishly scanning passersby, seemed to come out of the woodwork, and that evening the galleries of the Commons and the streets outside were filled with people hoping and expecting to see Riel take his seat.

Louis was no fool. His friends kept him informed of the hornet's nest his daring signature had stirred up, and he knew attempting to take his seat in Parliament would accomplish little more than his arrest. To the disappointment of the crowds, Riel stayed in Hull. Still, eager spectators of the political drama were not to be completely cheated. His appearance before Patrick prompted a heated debate over the Métis and their leader that exploded in the House. The newly elected majority Liberal government soundly defeated two Québec motions calling for an amnesty for Riel and the other Métis.

This was the same party, of course, that still had a standing $5000 bounty on Riel's head. The English side of the party was littered with prominent Orangemen, including one Mackenzie Bowell, member for the riding of Belleville, Ontario, who proposed a motion demanding "Louis Riel be ordered to attend the House tomorrow." The Liberals rammed the motion through the House, despite protests from French-Canadian members, thus presenting Riel with

A political cartoon that appeared in the magazine *Grip,* April 11, 1874, in which Louis Riel is depicted as a wanted man

a rather difficult decision. If he appeared to take his seat, he was sure to be arrested. Yet if he didn't, he would surely lose his seat. When Riel chose the latter, the one and only Honorable Member of Parliament John Schultz was only too happy to rise in the House and second Bowell's motion to expel Riel from Parliament.

Again there was some protest from French-Canadian members, but an overriding loyalty along party lines carried the motion to remove Riel with a generous majority. The victory was short lived, however, since the Liberals were forced to call yet another by-election for the riding of Provencher. There were some murmurs of opposition from the Métis community this time. Taché and a few of the more prominent and conservative Métis thought that it might be prudent to elect a member that could actually sit in the House and represent his constituents. This stung Louis, who had regained his stamina and was anxious to represent his people in Ottawa.

He wired his friend Joseph Dubuc in Manitoba: "Please see that they reelect me in Provencher; our cause is stronger than ever. I will fight for amnesty and the institution of a fair, responsible government."

The majority of Métis in Provencher agreed that Riel's cause was also theirs. Support for the disbanded MP swelled in Manitoba and Québec, where a "Manitoba Committee" was formed to support the campaign. And so the only candidate the Métis cared to nominate was again elected by acclamation for the riding of Provencher. Surely, his supporters felt, this third election in a row would force the federal government's hand on the issue of the oft-promised amnesty, which was now finally beginning to come into the public eye.

Louis published his thoughts on the issue in a pamphlet entitled *L'Amnestie*. The ensuing protest and turmoil prompted the government to set up a Special Committee on the Causes of the Difficulties in the North-West Territory. The committee garnered tremendous publicity as the press in Québec and Ontario devoted lavish space to the juicy testimony that emerged. But the spotlight was a double-edged sword for Riel. He found that the furore of attention increased fears for his safety, sending him taking flight once again.

Politically, though, the committee was nothing but good news for Riel. Archbishop Taché's testimony in particular seemed damning of the government. Taché, who had never stopped working within the system to procure the amnesty promised by Macdonald's government during the resistance, had a lot to say to the committee. When his opportunity to testify before the Special Committee arrived, Taché was relieved at the chance to go public with his side of the story. At long last, Canada finally heard about the private promises made to Taché and Ritchot of an amnesty for Riel and his followers. Macdonald responded by claiming that no such promises had ever been made, but it was obvious to all Canadians that their former prime minister was not being entirely honest.

The evidence seemed clear, but Riel remained the sharpest of political thorns. In spite of Taché's testimony, Orange Ontario still viewed Riel as a villain. All that the committee revealed to them was that Macdonald and Cartier had simply been wrong in promising amnesty. The issue simmered for a few more months, but Riel's persistence in Provencher and the notable lack of a representative in the House of Commons demanded action from Prime Minister Mackenzie. The fact that Ambroise Lépine's notoriously biased murder trial ended with a guilty verdict November 2, 1874, did little to ameliorate the urgency of the question of amnesty. Although Lépine's jury recommended mercy for the Métis leader, the judge still sentenced him to hang. Finally, on February 12, 1875, Prime Minister Alexander Mackenzie, under extreme pressure, rose in the House and motioned that amnesty be granted to all participants in the Red River Resistance with the exception of Riel and Lépine. Lépine's sentence was commuted to a two-year jail term, and Riel was to be expelled from Parliament and banished from all British territory for a period of five years. The Liberal majority carried the motion handily, passing it by a vote of 126–50.

While such a verdict must have been hard to swallow, some part of the beleaguered young man was relieved that the situation had been resolved. True, he had been pronounced guilty for standing up for his home and his people, but at least he could walk away knowing that his leadership had helped preserve that home and that people. His home and his people had become central to Louis over the course of the last few years. Deprived of them by Parliament, Louis would lose himself in dark introspection, devoting more and more of his energies to a complex and increasingly bizarre personal religion that would eventually lead him to madness.

CHAPTER EIGHT

Exile

LOUIS RIEL WAS SPINNING into a personal limbo. Having spent more than five years struggling for amnesty, the sudden and total disconnection from his homeland left a gaping hole in his life. Louis had invested too much time and effort, had fought too hard and sacrificed too much to simply walk away from the province he had fathered. Parliament's sentence of exile was a fierce blow to the young man, and the mere thought of the next half-decade away from his land and his people threw him into a deep depression.

Parliament's exile not only struck at the sensitive young man's heart, it also cut into his sense of self-worth. If Riel had proven anything during the Red River Resistance, it was that he possessed a prodigious talent in politics. He was charismatic and intelligent, an eloquent and rousing speaker and a gifted negotiator imbued with a remarkable ability to turn contention into consensus. Some might argue that Riel's passion and zealous sense of justice occasionally blinded him to the concerns of others, yet it was precisely his staunch belief in himself and his cause that made him such a convincing leader. Those who met Louis during his exile probably wouldn't have taken the disturbed young man for a leader of anything.

Wrought by longing, loneliness, resentment and regret, the exiled Riel became a shell of the person he once was.

Louis did not fall apart all at once. He had been known to lapse into sudden feverish deliriums during the stress of the Red River Resistance, and in the following years when he was a man on the run, he developed fervent religious ideas that were alarmingly unconventional. Yet it wasn't until after his 1875 exile that Louis' tortured psyche led him to complete madness.

The entire time he was falling, Riel clung with ever-increasing devotion to the one pillar that had always been central to his life: his Christian faith. Roman Catholic roots ran deep and strong in the Riel family. Louis' mother, Julie, had grown up intent on becoming a nun. When her parents proposed that she forsake a marriage to Christ for a more earthly union with Jean-Louis Riel she was adamantly against it until, that is, she received a stern and rather terrifying command from none other than the Almighty. According to family legend, God Himself descended to Julie a few days after she spurned young Jean-Louis' proposal. She was just leaving church when flames burst forth all around her, forming a roaring cage of flame that she dared not walk through. Dazzled and frightened, she raised her eyes to the heavens and saw there a majestic-looking man hovering among the clouds, flashing with light and encircled with fire. In her heart, she knew without a doubt that this was her God.

He spoke in a powerful voice, and his message was succinct: "Disobedient child, when you return to your home, you will tell your parents that you will obey them and marry the man who has been chosen for you."

This sort of dramatic mystical vision was not considered outlandish among the Métis, a people whose religious beliefs were shaped by a combination of Native American mysticism and traditional Catholic spirituality. The Métis faith was a heady combination of martyrs, miracles, visions and acts of devotion. For the most part, the Métis were a spiritual people who revered their priests and their formal religion as much as they did the spiritual allegories of their Native ancestors. Stories of flying canoes, vision quests and ghosts—malicious and benign—floated about the evening firesides. Omens and augury were to be found in everyday events; the flight of a bird or a gust of wind might suggest good fortune or coming calamity.

Louis was very much his mother's son, and he carried her fervent religious belief into the world with him.

"Family prayers, the rosary were always in my eyes and ears. And they are as much a part of my nature as the air I breathe," Riel later reminisced. His mother was blushingly proud of her eldest son's religious devotion, and she often told people that the first words out of his mouth when he was an infant were not "mommy" or "daddy" but "Jesus," "Mary" and "Joseph."

Louis' faith had remained unshakable throughout the course of his life. From his stern Catholic schooling to his struggles with a commitment to the priesthood to his everyday acts of piety, his great faith was always nestled in his breast. Throughout the Red River conflict, it had remained the one constant in his life amid the tumult and chaos of the resistance. Yet it was during the first year of his exile that, deprived of everything else, religion *became* Riel's life. The man that led Louis into this new and painful phase of his life was none other than the Bishop of Montréal, Ignace Bourget.

He had first met the Québec bishop in a Montréal hospital called the Hôtel-Dieu in January 1874, just before Riel's aborted attempt to take his seat in Parliament. Bourget was recuperating from a bad cold, and Riel was suffering from nervous exhaustion in the wake of the Red River troubles. The Hôtel-Dieu physicians could find nothing physically wrong with Riel, and the demoralized man was about to leave when he was told, offhand, that Bishop Bourget was recovering at the hospital. Convinced that his sickness was some sort of spiritual malady, Louis requested an audience with the exalted priest. The bedridden bishop agreed to see him.

Awestruck, Riel's heart began pounding the moment he walked into the bishop's room. In Louis' mind, he may as well have been speaking to a saint. He began to speak when the strain of the previous years washed over him in a sudden wave. An instant later, he was barely able to restrain his tears.

Louis fell to his knees at the foot of Bourget's bed saying, "Please, Father, help me. I am sick."

Old Bourget tried to sit up in his bed but was unable. "Arise, arise," Bourget responded wearily. "You are going to recover your health. Do what your doctor prescribes. I will be sure to bless the medicines that are given to you."

That was all it took. Just over a week later, Riel felt much like his old self, once more determined to take on whatever forces were arrayed against him for the interests of his people. Of course, he attributed his sudden recovery to the miracle of the bishop's blessing.

The experience stuck with Riel, and he wrote a letter of thanks to Bourget a year later: "With God's grace, I will always remember with gratitude the life-giving words you spoke to me at the Hôtel-Dieu."

And so on July 6, 1875, after receiving the cruel news of his banishment, Riel, flailing once more in dark eddies of doubt and depression, wrote Bourget for guidance. "I come and throw myself humbly at your feet," he wrote to the bishop, "to assure you that I want to spend my life in the dust at God's feet, humble in heart and body."

And although the bishop may have been trying to help, his subsequent messianic response only hurtled Riel into a destructive cycle of self-centered delusion:

I have a deep conviction that you will be rewarded in this world, and sooner than you expect, for the inner sacrifices you have made which are a thousand times more painful than sacrifices of material and visible things. God, who has up until the present directed you and assisted you, will not abandon you in your most difficult of struggles, for He has given you a mission which you must accomplish step by step and with the Grace of God you must persevere on the path that has been laid out for you.

If Bourget thought that his words would lend Riel some much-needed peace, he was wrong. Louis took the words as a carte blanche to listen to his own inner compulsions, which, as Bourget himself wrote, were directions from God.

Riel was reminded that his arduous journey through this veil of tears was all a part of His divine plan, and that Riel had the honor of being selected to play a central role in His celestial scheme. These were words that Bourget wholeheartedly believed. He would later confide to Father Albert Lacombe that he viewed Riel as an "instrument of providence."

The bishop's faith in the Métis leader was not taken lightly. Louis was so profoundly affected by Bourget's words that he carried the letter in his vest pocket over his heart until the day he died. By casting Riel as an important figure in God's divine plan, Bourget flattered Louis' considerable ego while providing direction and purpose to a man lost amid pain, bewilderment and frustration.

Finding the strength to act after receiving Bourget's letter, Riel began scheming his next political play: an invasion into western Canada. It was a desperate plan, but Riel felt confident that he had God on his side. The Canadian government had continued to drag its heels on the issue of Métis land distribution and seemed reluctant to live up to the spirit of the treaties it was signing with various tribes of Plains Natives. Believing that he could count on Métis discontent with Canadian rule in Manitoba, recalcitrant Native tribes that were friendly with his people and his own personal influence in the region, Riel thought that he had a good chance at wresting control of the region from Ottawa's grasp. And perhaps he could have, if not for his dependence on the United States.

The plan was to foment an uprising amongst the settlers and force Canada to renegotiate a new independent republic west of Manitoba where Saskatchewan is today. Canada had a weak military presence in the region at the time: a tiny, questionable militia and the newly arrived, widely scattered North-West Mounted Police. These forces were perhaps sufficient to deal with a small-scale riot, but not a full-fledged uprising. And this time, if the Canadians did send an army westward, Riel was determined not to be so trusting or pacific.

Yet the one vital prerequisite for an occupation of the Canadian West by Riel was support from the United States. He needed sufficient financing, permission to openly use U. S. territory as a base of operations and a guarantee that Canadian troops would be prohibited from using the American railways to bring reinforcements to Red River. In his zealous enthusiasm, Riel may have convinced himself that the U.S. government would be receptive to his plan. In October 1875, he sat down with Indiana Senator Oliver P. Morton—a prominent Republican politician who was famous for championing the downtrodden—and presented the proposal. Riel knew from the moment he opened his mouth that the Americans would not back him. Morton didn't mince any words when he told Louis that the United States wouldn't be willing to risk war with the British Empire for the formation of Louis' republic. Though Senator Morton wasn't in a position to offer an authoritative statement to Louis' proposal, the meeting went poorly enough to discourage him from pursuing his plan any further.

A dejected Louis Riel left Indianapolis and traveled to Washington, D.C., where he lived with a friend named Edmond Mallet. In December 1875, not long after he arrived in Washington, Riel received the one bit of news from Red River that would prove to be his undoing. His little brother, Charles, had died after battling a fever for nearly a month. Riel had seen little of his brother as he matured from youth into manhood, and he knew that Charles had sacrificed his education at an early age to work to support his family. He had been working on a railway gang when he came down with the fever that killed him. Riel must have been filled with regrets as he wondered how things might have been different if only he'd had the ability to support his family.

"My dear brother Meunier," Riel confided with ink and paper, using his pet name for his little brother, "how his death has caused me pain."

It was at this point that Louis Riel began to lose his grip on reality. In mid-December, he made a desperate visit to President Grant at the White House, hoping to sell his scheme of an independent republic in Western Canada. And although his reputation as the Métis leader did get him an audience, Grant flatly rejected the idea. This was the final blow. His host, Edmond Mallet, could not help noticing Riel's declining condition.

"He was easily polite to the few persons he met—my wife, children, sister-in-law and a few choice friends," Mallet would later remember. But this pleasant demeanor was a shell. "He would not go into society," Mallet recalled. "He went to Mass every morning and crept into some dark spot in some church at night to recite his evening prayers."

While in Washington, after losing his brother and his cause, Riel retreated even deeper into his inner religious world where he was the prophet inspired by Bishop Bourget's letter, whose suffering would—hope of all hopes—one day be vindicated. Yet nothing in the immediate present suggested anything of the sort. Socially isolated and emotionally devastated, praying for nothing less than divine intervention to deliver him from the daily torment his life had become, Louis Riel's world began to take a different shape through his ardent eyes.

Attending Mass that December, Riel experienced a revelation: "I suddenly felt in my heart a joy which so possessed me that to hide the smile on my face from my neighbors I had to unfold my handkerchief and hold it with my hand over my mouth and cheeks," he later recalled. "After rejoicing thus for about two minutes, I immediately felt an immense sadness of the soul. And if I had not made a great effort to contain my sobs, my cries and my tears would have exploded throughout the church. For discretion's sake, I bore in silence the almost intolerable sadness that I was feeling in my soul. But that great pain, that had been as great as my joy, passed in a while. And my spirit rang with one thought: the joys and the sorrows of man here on earth are but brief."

He wrote a confused and disturbing letter to Edmond Mallet that same day. Disjointed, switching from English to French and back again in mid-sentence, the letter was an exuberant tirade about one of the Mallets' maids, whom Riel compared to the Virgin Mary. From there, his letter broke into a paranoid rant about the possibilities of thieves or spies breaking into his room and stealing his treasured cache of documents. There is no evidence, however, that anyone was after Riel at this time. Mallet had begun to suspect that Riel had gone insane.

It seems that Riel's state of mind was evolving into an extreme dementia, and it wasn't long before he was no longer able to get along with the people around him. Mallet, a heretofore-loyal friend, suddenly felt that he and his family could bear Louis' presence in their home no longer. In the space of a few weeks, Riel was passed from the home of his good friend, to his priest and confessor, to yet another priest, Father Barnabé, and finally, to his uncle John Lee in Montréal. No one, not even family, was able to bear Louis' presence for more than a few days. The accumulated pressures of the last half decade had finally taken their toll as Louis' mind succumbed to madness.

During the winter of 1875–76, Riel openly insisted that he was a prophet and sometimes even boasted that he was the Messiah—the Son of God. He begged to be allowed to proclaim it publicly. On other occasions, he saw himself as one of a trinity of monarchs kept from their rightful thrones—the Bourbon king in France and Don Carlos of Spain being the other two. In Louis' mind, each king came to be represented by a different colored flag and a bull: black for the Bourbon, white for Carlos and red for Riel (representing the blood that Christ and Christian martyrs had shed). At times Louis even snorted, pawed the ground and roared, becoming the bull his fevered mind had fabricated, much to the chagrin of his horrified hosts.

He went for days without sleep. He would pace, agitated, for hours on end. He let loose bone-chilling cries and howls at all hours. In the words of his uncle, he "had contortions like a man in a rage." He locked himself in his room and tore his clothing and bedding to tatters. After the madness had passed, someone had to dress him again while the suddenly calm Riel waited patiently, almost like a child. These moments of calm lucidity made it even harder on those around him, who believed that some part of Riel was still sane. At times he could even carry on a normal conversation, but if his companions ever tentatively broached the topic of his obvious mental instability, Riel's madness would boil to the surface.

"No, I am not crazy!" he yelled at anyone who suggested it. "I have a mission to perform, and I am a prophet. I am sent by God!"

Each of his caretakers came to a similar conclusion. After Riel spent a few days with Father Primeau, the priest thought that nothing but a miracle could restore Louis to "his normal state." The priest obviously didn't have much faith in miracles, though, for he also prayed that Louis might meet an honorable end before too long. When Riel's uncle arrived at Keeseville to collect his nephew, he couldn't believe his eyes when he saw how haggard and spent Father Barnabé looked.

"What's wrong?" he asked the priest immediately.

"Poor Louis!" Barnabé responded. "He is out of his mind!"

Then, after a few months of enduring Louis' erratic behavior, the Lees, who had smuggled their banished nephew across the Canadian border in a privately hired carriage, were at their wits' end. They decided to have Riel committed. Louis never would have agreed to it, so they tricked him, telling him that they were going for a carriage ride out in the country when in fact they were headed for the gates of Longue-Point, an insane asylum not far from Montréal. Riel never forgave his uncle for the deception.

Committed on March 6, 1876, Louis spent the next two years of his life in insane asylums as his psychosis continued to worsen. Registered as "Louis David" while in Longue-Point to protect both him and the reputation of the institution, Louis spent his time there grappling with those who policed the boundaries of sanity.

He was a difficult patient. One of his favorite stunts was to parade about in the nude. Most times he felt constrained by clothing, and he would calmly take his clothes off, but on other occasions he would angrily rip the garments off his back and tear his bedding to shreds.

In a letter to Father Bourget, he explained his penchant for nudity in surprising eloquence for a madman. "The spirit of charity told me, 'The one who is good must show himself naked. Because he is beautiful,'" Louis wrote. "'The one who disobeys is the one who must hide himself. Because he is ugly.' Afterwards, the good Lord said: 'In truth, in truth, the day is coming when all men will stand up naked from the bowels of earth.'" It is a testament to the bishop's sway over Riel that a letter from Bourget asking him to stop was all it took to curb this spiritually inspired exhibitionism.

Often violent and incomprehensible, Louis suffered through extreme delusions of grandeur. Once, while visiting Longue-Point's chapel for prayer, Louis became enraged with how dirty the room was. He bellowed and flailed his arms in fury, sending candles and linens flying in great sweeps.

He even broke the glass of the chapel door in his self-righteous rage, roaring, "Louis David will not speak with his father in such a filthy hovel!"

He began to sign his private writings "Louis David Riel, Prophet, Infallible Pontiff, Priest King." He experienced curious, mystical visions. "I saw a turtle. I said: 'Lord what does this mean?' And the Lord answered: 'This is the government of Ottawa that walks like a turtle.'" At one point, he demanded to consecrate his own meal as the flesh and blood of Christ.

Perhaps this was Riel's way of dealing with the godly mission that Bourget had bestowed upon him in that fateful letter. His fragile mind interpreted the well-intentioned bishop's ministering in a way that Bourget could have never expected.

"The Holy Spirit," he wrote to Bourget, "pushes me with one hand and holds me back with the other so strongly that I feel that I'm being crushed by a mountain at the same time as I leap into action on the wings of my mission."

Locked in the grim confines of an insane asylum, Riel may have wondered if this was the greater sacrifice to which the Bishop had urged him.

As difficult as it was, Riel made the most of his time in the asylum, developing even stranger theories about his place in the world. He imagined the Natives as one of the lost tribes of Israel and himself a contemporary embodiment of the biblical King David. Before long, Bishop Bourget would be the new pope and Montréal appointed the new Rome. Somehow, Riel calculated that in 2333 AD, his home of St. Vital would become the seat of authority for a renewed Catholic Church that had successfully completed its proper migration from the Old World to the New. While he was confined, he believed all of these theories with an unshakable certainty.

Riel stepped off the map of accepted 19th-century spiritualism and delved into a realm of self-created religious delusion. Yet if Riel's insane musings were an attempt to escape a reality that was too hard to face, the conditions at Longue-Point hardly made Louis' reality any easier to bear. Tragically typical of insane asylums in the 19th century, Longue-Point was a cold, filthy, overcrowded hovel that was governed with brutal discipline. The operating principle in Longue-Point was the belief that a lack of inner discipline made the insane what they were, and that if patients were subjected to rigid daily routines, they might be cured of their conditions. Next to no activity was permitted outside Longue-Point's institutionalized routines, and the price for recalcitrance was high. When Louis protested loudly after his valise of correspondence, personal documents and writing materials had been taken away without a word of warning or explanation, he was stripped naked and restrained in a straightjacket.

A few years after Riel's stay there, a visiting British physician described Longue-Point as one of the most depressing asylums he had ever seen in his 37 years of experience in the field. Proclaiming the asylum a "chamber of horrors," he compared the individual cells to animal pens entirely unadorned and narrow, with hardly space for a bed. The only natural light entered through a small opening in the doorway, which the handlers opened and closed at will. Money was tight, so the food was generally on par with gruel. It was, in short, little wonder that Riel showed little improvement at Longue-Point, and he pleaded with Bourget in regular correspondence, begging the priest to get him out.

After being moved to a somewhat better institution in Beauport, near Québec City, during the early summer of 1876, Riel's condition slowly began to improve. Having his valise returned to him, Louis plunged into writing as a form of therapy. In his diaries, the normally polite man lashed out with bitter sarcasm at those whom he judged to have betrayed him and the Métis cause. Railing against those individuals and institutions, his writings in Beauport were one angry tirade after another. His writing was prolific, and as it turned out, a sorely needed outlet for the demons that troubled him.

Nor were his writings limited to his journal. By post, he renewed contact with family and friends. The love and support that flowed back to him must have been a tonic.

"The sooner you become submissive and obedient," his good friend Father Barnabé wrote back to him in good priestly form, "the sooner you will find good health and the sooner it will be the pleasure of your friends to find you among them again."

Riel agreed. In the early summer of 1876, he wrote to Bourget, admitting that he had a problem and stressing a desire to be cured. The admission was a huge step on the road to his recovery.

On January 29, 1878, the authorities at Beauport released Riel. Wary of the Orange storm they might summon if it was discovered that Riel had secretly been in Canada for the past two years, they smuggled him back across the border into the United States. Having finally defeated the demons of failure and disappointment, Louis Riel was free once again, a free man in a free world, left alone to make his way as he saw fit, as long as he stayed south of the 49th parallel.

CHAPTER NINE

Reunion

RIEL LEFT BEAUPORT ASYLUM and Canada; he was a changed man moving into a changed world. The cause he had devoted himself to for so many years, the world that had driven him to madness, these were now in a past that Louis was trying his best to leave undisturbed. Shutting out his provenance from his mind, Riel stood before an uncertain and rather frightening future. Exiled, devoid of direction and practically penniless, Louis was less than enthusiastic about his new lease on life. Thankfully, he had good friends to turn to.

Remembering the kindness of the Barnabé family in the fall of 1873, just before he went to Ottawa to claim his parliamentary seat, Riel traveled straight to Keeseville, New York, where he was reunited with Father Fabien Barnabé and his beautiful sister, Evelina. Louis had been through a lot in the five years since he had last seen his friend's sister, but in all that time, he had never quite forgotten her.

Evelina Barnabé was a thin, delicate woman with pretty features, blonde hair and blue eyes. She was well read, intelligent and fluent with the issues and doctrines of her religion. Louis quickly fell in love with this thoughtful and devout Catholic woman, whose kind attentions and hospitality made her a ministering angel to the broken Riel.

The rebellious, fiery-eyed Métis certainly captured young Evelina's heart. Well-mannered and sophisticated, Louis was just the sort of gentleman who appealed to Evelina's refined tastes. Yet underneath his well-kept veneer, she sensed a passion, foreign and impetuous, that was bred somewhere beyond the western horizon in a world she had never known. There was just enough prairie in Louis Riel to lend him a streak of frontier romance—an air of noble tragedy. On many occasions, Evelina imagined she saw a wild spark flash in Louis' dark eyes, turning the gentle young man into some-one she couldn't recognize. And then there was his past: his skill and the sacrifice he made on behalf of his people evoked admiration in the young woman; his unjust suffering and emotional turmoil evoked her sympathy. It wasn't long before the sheltered woman found herself dreaming of a life with the Barnabés' dramatic young guest.

They grew closer with each passing day. Sharing intense conver-sations at the dinner table, running errands together around town and going on long walks through the countryside, Louis and Evelina cultivated a deep bond. Just as he had done when he became enam-ored with Marie Guernon so many years ago, Louis began courting Evelina with surreptitious love letters. He composed laudatory poems, where he heaped stacks of flattering adjectives on the object of his desire. She returned his affections.

"Please accept as a souvenir for your birthday, these flowers. You will find among them an oleander," she wrote him in the summer of 1878. "It is an emblem of my vital and sincere love."

Evelina's mother, however, wasn't able to forget how difficult Riel's lunacy had been on their family and made it known that she did not approve of the match. This was nothing new for Louis, who was also spurned by Marie Guernon's parents because of his mixed-blood her-itage. Undeterred, the couple made a secret pledge to marry.

Louis may have been wealthy in love during his time with the Barnabés, but he could not live on sentiment alone. He made himself as useful as he could that summer, doing odd jobs around the house, but at the end of the day, he was still dependent on the family's charity. An intelligent, physically healthy man, Louis quite naturally believed that he should be making his own way in the world. He knocked on doors and pondered various avenues, going as far as New York City, hoping to find work as a journalist or law clerk, yet remarkably, the well-educated 34-year-old could find no lasting employment.

By the fall of 1878, Riel abandoned hope of making a living in New York, and like so many other American men at the time, he began to contemplate the opportunities in the wide-open West. He did not deliberate for long. In late November, Louis bid the generous Barnabés farewell, assuring his tearful betrothed that he would send for her as soon as he had established himself. And then he was gone, back to the West, arriving in St. Paul just in time for Christmas. For over half a year, he drifted from one settlement to the next, moving from Minnesota to the Dakota Territory, relying on a network of Métis friends and family for work and shelter. In the summer of 1879, Riel joined a group of Métis buffalo hunters in Montana Territory. It was there, on a rough Métis settlement near Beaver Creek, just south of the Frenchman River, that Riel made his new home.

Life in Montana Territory was harsh. Only the toughest could endure the brutal winters, with the vicious blizzards that sliced over the land like frozen scythes. Louis had endured no small measure of difficulty in his life, but this was his first experience with the traditional Métis dependence on the buffalo hunt. Métis existence in the West had always been difficult and precarious, and only got worse when the buffalo herds began to dwindle. When Louis arrived in Montana, the buffalo were almost gone, and the little community on Beaver Creek was in the throes of unprecedented poverty. Conditions in the Métis settlement were about as bad as the frontier could be. The community was plagued by the sort of whiskey-soaked

Louis Riel, when he was living in Montana around 1883

violence that made the American West the stuff of legend. While
Riel waxed religious against the widespread drunkenness in the settlement, his public denunciations made little difference to the coarse
breed of men who lived in the area. All the while, Riel despaired at
the thought of his frail and delicate fiancée, raised on tea parties and
parlor proprieties, moving to his new Montana home. The idea
seemed more and more ludicrous with each passing month, until

Louis finally accepted that his fiancée could never enjoy a happy life with him on the fringes of the U.S.

Evelina herself had expressed doubts to Riel, telling him in letters that she might prove to be an embarrassment to him, that she lacked the courage to thrive in such a harsh existence. Thrive or survive? Riel must have wondered. Eventually deciding that bringing Evelina west would be the equivalent of sentencing her to a sure and cruel death, he stopped corresponding with her.

By all accounts, Riel barely missed his former fiancée, so absorbed did he become in the struggle for survival on the frontier. Louis had always been a prolific correspondent, but almost none of his friends or family heard from him throughout much of 1880 and 1881. Indeed, Evelina Barnabé was still under the impression that she and Louis were engaged to be married, only learning that her betrothed had taken another woman for his wife when she opened a western newspaper and read the announcement that Louis Riel and Marguerite Monet dit Bellehumeur had been wed.

Louis met Marguerite during the long, dark winter of 1880. The pretty young Métis woman enchanted him from the very moment he set eyes on her. Though she was 16 years his junior, Marguerite was hardly a frivolous youth. The hard environment had aged her early, imbuing her with a stoic seriousness and unflinching resourcefulness that transcended her years. Theirs was a simple courtship, devoid of fanciful trappings and expressions of lofty sentiments, but Louis still found the time for poetic expression, writing his now-customary odes on feminine charm to his latest inspiration.

He asked Marguerite's father, Jean-Baptiste, for his daughter's hand in February 1881. They were married on April 28, 1881. There was no priest present, so the ceremony was conducted *a la façon du pays* (in the custom of the country), their wedding vows solemnized by Marguerite's father. After so many years of trouble and uncertainty, Riel turned his attention to making himself a home.

In May 1882, Marguerite gave birth to a son. They named him Jean, and the beaming young infant became a wellspring of joy for

The soft-spoken Marguerite Monet (1861–88) was married to Louis when she was 20 years old. They had two children together.

Louis. Hoping to provide a steady income, Riel moved his young family to the tiny frontier community of St. Peter's Mission in the spring of 1883, where he took up a job as a teacher in a small rustic school run by the local Jesuits. But even as Louis began to settle down, he felt the ghosts of his past tugging at him.

A few weeks after he arrived in St. Peter's, Riel became a U.S. citizen. Experiencing what he described as a "moral sadness" when he received his citizenship, Louis had difficulty coming to terms with the fact that he had left his homeland behind him. Try as he might to forget, Louis still thought of the Red River Métis often, floundering in still waters of regret and remorse when he did. Perhaps it was in an effort to forget that Louis threw himself into the work around him with renewed vigor. He became a dedicated and effective teacher, taking personal interest in the development of each of his students. The locals weren't used to such diligence from their instructors, and one student's mother expressed her appreciation in a letter of thanks to St. Peter's eager new teacher.

"Many heartfelt thanks from a devoted mother for all the kindness you have shown my children," she wrote.

In September 1883, Marguerite gave birth to a girl, whom the couple christened Marie-Angélique. If the parents were grateful for the blessing of another child, Marie was also another mouth to feed, and given Louis' meager income and the tiny cabin they called home, the Riels' lives came to be defined by challenge and hardship. Marguerite worked around the clock caring for her two infants, tending to the family's modest plot of land and trying to make their simple cabin into a home. Meanwhile, Riel struggled with the knowledge that, despite all his dedication to his students, he still wasn't earning enough to give his wife and children the life he would have liked.

His thoughts turned regularly to the past, and he dwelt bitterly on the years of the Red River Resistance, where all the reward he got for his work in the provisional government was exile and torment. More and more, he lingered over the debt he thought was owed to him. These tortured musings led Riel back to questions of God, of the perceived mission that was laid out before him and of the fate of his people—all queries that had once already taken him to the fringes of sanity. Ever so slowly, he started down that path again.

Riel began to be disturbed by visions and haunting dreams; sometimes he claimed to have seen his father drifting across his property; on other occasions, he had casual conversations with the Holy Spirit. He festered on questions of his purpose on earth, alternating between a brimming confidence and forlorn questioning.

"Who am I?" he privately vented his doubts. "Who am I to attempt to lead events?"

The tumultuous times of the Red River Resistance must have seemed like a past life to Louis Riel, now wearing the mantle of a humble schoolmaster. Louis' underlying problem was that, despite all his efforts at meekness, his oversized ego and ambition would not let him remain a teacher in a tiny frontier settlement.

Early on the morning of June 4, 1884, another opportunity at greatness came knocking. One of St. Peter's parishioners interrupted Riel's volunteer duties during Mass, whispering to him that four strangers had just arrived outside the church and wished to speak with him. A little annoyed at having his Mass interrupted, Riel quietly left the church and stepped out into the bright spring morning. Four dusty men, clearly tired from long travel, waited a short distance away. The moment he stepped outside, one of the four strode forward to meet him.

He was a middle-aged man, his dark hair and beard peppered with gray. Yet it was clear from his powerful build and muscular stride that the approaching stranger had lost none of his vigor to age. Indeed, the firm look in his dark, steady eyes suggested that his years had only imbued him with deeper strength. Everything about this man bespoke power, from the steely expression on his rugged, sun-browned face, to the way he carried his short, broad frame. He stood no taller than 5'8", but the breadth of his enormous shoulders made him look like a giant.

He stopped before Louis and held out a heavily callused hand. "Hello, Monsieur Riel," he spoke with a gruff French tongue, "me and my companions have traveled a long way to meet you."

Riel nodded and smiled politely. "I can see that, but I'm afraid you have me at a disadvantage. For while you seem to know who I am, I can't say the same of you."

"Pardon me," the big man said. "You do not know me, but I'm sure you've heard my name. I am Gabriel Dumont."

St. Peter's Mission, Montana, where Louis Riel was a school-teacher from 1883 to 1884

Riel didn't say anything for a few long moments, caught completely off-guard by the newcomer's introduction. Of course he had heard of Gabriel Dumont! Every Canadian west of the 100th meridian knew about the legendary Métis warrior who was said to be as deadly with a rifle as he was skillful in the saddle. He was the fiercely independent leader of the Métis community in the St. Laurent region, on the South Saskatchewan River. For a few seconds, Riel felt as if he must be staring at a statue, so celebrated was Gabriel Dumont in Métis culture.

"Of course, I know your name well," Riel replied with an uneasy smile, chuckling awkwardly. "Who hasn't heard your name?"

"Well then, we're on common ground," Gabriel responded. "I know of you as well and have come here to talk about matters north of the border."

As intrigued as Louis was, he was also painfully conscious of the fact that Mass was going on without him. Riel never missed Mass.

"Monsieur Dumont, of course I am interested in hearing what you have to say, but whatever it is, I'm sure that the word of the Lord takes precedence. I hope you will allow me to finish Mass before we continue."

Louis gave Dumont directions to his home, telling the Métis leader that he would meet him there shortly. Riel took one more look at Dumont walking back to his retinue before heading back into the church.

As surprised as Riel was by the visit, he had some idea why Dumont was there. For Riel knew that things hadn't been going well for the Métis recently. News of their continuing struggle for land and recognition had trickled to Riel over the years. Friends and family had made periodic visits to his humble home since he had returned to the West. Louis had even made a trip up to Winnipeg in 1883 to celebrate the wedding of his sister, Henriette. Amid the joy of reunion, however, Louis quickly became aware of a strong undercurrent of discontent.

Ottawa, it seemed, was not making good on the promises it had made in the Manitoba Act. Despite Macdonald's assurances to the contrary, land distribution to the Métis living in Red River had been neither speedy nor simple. After years of delay, the Dominion government finally decided that the 1.4 million acres allocated to the Métis to extinguish their Native title were not to be the valuable riverfront lots—where the Métis had traditionally settled but now coveted by incoming Canadians—but out in the middle of the prairie. In Métis eyes this land was next to worthless, and many of them ended up selling their "scrip," as the paper title came to be called, for as little as $25.

In the meantime, newly arrived settlers were allowed to stake and register claims on any vacant land, while older settlers were compelled to wait until a thorough survey of the homesteading land was completed prior to registering their ancestral, if unwritten, holdings. It was a nasty double standard that worked expressly against the Métis. Moreover, through a series of suspicious and quite possibly illegal inside moves, the Dominion government also changed the wording of the Manitoba Act to favor those land claimants with a more settled lifestyle. While significant improvements to homesteading plots—such as the construction of fences and barns—were necessary for the Métis to hold onto their lands, claimants also had to prove that they had been present on their lands on July 15, 1870, when the Manitoba Bill was enacted. However, this was the time of year when many would have been away hunting buffalo. Both were insidious blows against the semi-nomadic, buffalo-hunting Métis, who often found that there was little in the way of material proof that tied them to the lands they claimed as their own.

The Métis lost out on much of the land they had fought for, and that they had believed they had won, in the Manitoba Act of 1870. The problem wasn't the land alone. It was also the flood of settlers that washed over it. In just 15 years, the population in Red River grew to almost 10 times greater than it had been during the resistance. The Métis were reduced to a mere seven percent of the population. And, as many of the Métis leaders foresaw, the lack of established Métis "islands" of settlement left them more vulnerable to the coming tide of Protestant, English-speaking immigrants.

The Métis grievances did not stem so much from the fact that the Métis had lost their familiar majority in the community; rather, they were born from the attitude of the new majority. The shenanigans of Schultz and Mair, the inflammatory opinions of the *Nor'Wester*, the establishment of an Orange Lodge and Schultz's mob rule tactics in getting elected to the House of Commons—these had not been good omens of the coming Canadian population. Indeed, the arrival of the new wave of bigoted Manitobans just encouraged the Métis to sell their scrip at good prices or bad and leave.

But leave to where? Farther west, along the banks of the South Saskatchewan River, a small community of Métis led by the redoubtable Gabriel Dumont still clung to the familiar ways of the buffalo hunt, and many gravitated towards these Métis. But even here, the expanding mass of European populations could only be avoided for so long.

There were still some buffalo herds in these more westerly ranges, though they were sorry fragments compared to the massive numbers that used to graze over the Plains. Yet around 1880, with a surprising swiftness that shocked almost everyone, these too vanished. Even as Métis hunters, desperate for sustenance, shot the last buffalo, English settlers began their migration into the area, establishing communities at Battleford and Prince Albert.

The Métis were not blind to the irrepressible changes creeping into their lives. They had done their best to adapt. Under the leadership of Dumont, the community had established a modest form of self-government that had, among other things, legislated buffalo conservation measures, hoping to slow down the eradication of their primary resource for survival. However, the key concern once again was land. The move towards farming was not welcome among such a robust and proud hunting people as the Métis, but with their prey vanishing, they had to face the fact that they had no other option. The plow took the place of the musket, as mixed farms became larger and more common in Métis settlements.

While they had become increasingly dependent upon their small farms, the Métis still felt little security in their title. Surveyors moving through the West made it clear that the government was intent on imposing their inflexible grid upon the land. The system threatened the Métis in two respects. First, as in Red River, the Métis had marked out and operated their farms in their traditional manner—

Métis hunters rode specially trained horses called buffalo runners, and they followed the chief hunter as close to the herd as possible without being detected. They then fanned out to the right and left. Within 300 yards the buffalo usually became aware of the hunters' presence and began to move. The chief called "trot," and the men began a slow gallop. When the chief called "equa," they attacked the herd, and the running of the buffalo was in full force. For the uninitiated bystander, this process would certainly have appeared chaotic. Stampeding buffalo and swiftly moving horses, cloaked in clouds of dust, danced with a background of thundering hooves, bellowing buffalo, shouting Métis and cracking gunfire.

narrow strips of riverfront land. It was system of land distribution that did not mesh with the Canadian homesteading squares. Second, sections of land had been arbitrarily assigned to the railroad, to the Hudson's Bay Company and to schools. Some overlapped existing Métis holdings. The common question arising from both threats was: would the Métis holdings be respected? The Métis had no idea, but salivating land speculators moving through the region, trying to buy large blocks of land, whether it was occupied or not, only fed their fears. Throughout the early 1880s, the Métis had repeatedly petitioned Ottawa for official recognition of title to their lands. Each time they were ignored, even though the Dominion government had the explicit authority, under its own legislation, to make exceptions to the square land parceling in order to alleviate legitimate Métis concerns.

By the spring of 1884 their frustrations with the Dominion government had come to a head. After a series of meetings between local Métis and Half-breeds, it was decided that they required a more vigorous voice if Ottawa was to hear their concerns. They needed Louis Riel. He was chosen for the same reasons he took the leadership at Red River in the late 1860s. His education, character, political savvy and educational background made him a unique cultural bridge, a man who could be an advocate for Métis concerns in Ottawa's rarified political discourse. Riel was an obvious choice to lead Métis efforts in a negotiation with the East. Dumont and his three envoys departed from the banks of the South Saskatchewan River to take their petition to Riel.

After church on June 4, Riel sat and listened as Dumont voiced the concerns of his community. Word of this latest round of injustices against his people stirred Louis' blood.

"We need your help, Monsieur Riel," Gabriel rumbled. "You are the only one who has managed to get anything out of Ottawa."

Riel tried to disguise his pleasure, but the idea of the mighty Gabriel Dumont coming all this way to ask for his help made him flush with pride. And while he instinctively knew that he couldn't refuse his brethren's entreaty, Louis was careful not to jump in too hastily.

"Give me one night to pray on the matter, brother," Riel said to Gabriel. "You will have my answer first thing tomorrow."

The next morning, Gabriel Dumont was standing in front of the Riel family's cabin, silently watching the morning light fill the sky when Louis approached.

"It's an incredible sight, no?" Louis asked when he reached Gabriel's side.

The big man didn't take his eyes off the sky but shrugged and grunted an unintelligible response. After a moment or two of silence, he spoke.

"So, have you made up your mind?"

Riel's sigh was barely audible. "It has been 15 years since I gave my heart to my country," he said to the burly buffalo hunter. "And I am ready to give it again."

Gabriel turned to Louis and offered his hand. Riel took it. "If that is the case, we have much work to do."

By June 10, Riel, Marguerite and their two children had all their possessions packed into a Red River cart and were beginning their journey north to Canada, accompanied by Dumont and the three other Saskatchewan Métis. Riel had promised his wife that they would be back in Montana by September of that year, thinking that he would only help unite the Métis under their common cause and draft a petition that Ottawa would not be able to ignore. That was what he thought, not knowing how the situation in Batoche would unravel after he arrived there.

During the trip, Riel found his Métis escorts to be more than affable, and a firm bond developed between the voluble Riel and the rather stoic Gabriel Dumont. Louis talked most of the time, speaking about Christian spirituality. For the most part Dumont listened in silence, interrupting only occasionally to point out natural landmarks, animal tracks or tell a short hunting story. They were very different men, practically opposites, yet their differences did nothing to stop a mutual respect from developing. By the time they reached trail's end, Riel and Dumont were fast friends.

The warmth of this simple friendship did not prepare Louis for the overwhelming welcome he received as he approached the South Saskatchewan settlements. Word that Riel was nearing had preceded him, and as the traveling party pulled up to the Couteau family's farm at Fish Creek, it was greeted in stunningly grand fashion.

Sixty wagons full of men, women and children had come to greet him. A celebratory *feu de joie* was sent thundering into the skies along with old patriotic songs. Louis Riel had no idea what kind of impact his 1869 stand against Ottawa had made on the Metis people. Many had only heard of him, the heroic figure that had fought so hard and well for the Métis some 15 years before at Red River. Young and old alike wanted to meet this great man. They lined up to shake his hand, give him their thanks and shout their encouragement. Riel recognized some old friends from Red River among the assembled throng in the Métis settlement. He spotted his cousin and former adversary, Charles Nolin, in the welcoming committee.

"Charles?" Louis asked tentatively, a little unsure about what to say to the man who had turned against him in 1869.

He received a boisterous shout from Nolin. "Louis!" In another moment, the two cousins threw their arms around each other in joyful reconciliation.

Bygones were bygones in the optimistic atmosphere that descended over Batoche that summer, and Louis accepted Nolin's offer to stay at his house. There he delivered a brief speech to a crowd of Métis supporters on July 8. Hesitant to say too much about a situation that he still hadn't had a chance to investigate thoroughly, Riel was humble, even understated. He merely stressed that unity was required of everyone in the region if they were to be successful.

He set to work immediately, getting to know the grievances of the Métis who lived along the South Saskatchewan. Riel quickly decided upon a similar strategy to that which he had pursued in Red River, building a broad coalition and approaching Ottawa with a

Batoche as it appeared shortly after the North-West Rebellion of 1885

united front when presenting its petition. Hoping to get the English-speaking settlers on board with his movement, Riel attended a meeting of English-speaking farmers in a schoolhouse on Red Deer Hill. Standing at his side throughout the meeting was Gabriel Dumont.

The region's English community had grown to be just as upset with the Dominion government as the Métis were. Poor harvests brought on by years of drought and early frost were compounded by Canada's 1883 economic crash, when wheat prices fell dramatically. So it wasn't too difficult for Louis, who spoke to these farmers with the same easy tone he had used on July 8, to convince them to fall in line with the Métis protest.

Another meeting was held in the town of Prince Albert on July 19, where Louis addressed a packed hall in the bustling community on the North Saskatchewan River. Word of his arrival had spread throughout the entire North-West, and people came from near and far to hear what the deposed Métis leader had to say. For his part, Louis was all too conscious of the volatility of the situation as he addressed over 500 North-West residents—English and French— in the packed Prince Albert Hall. Again, he left his theatrics at home and delivered a statement on moderation and unity. He made it clear that he wasn't preaching revolution or resistance, just for Ottawa to recognize the grievances of the people of the North-West.

The crowd responded to his speech enthusiastically, and every-thing would have gone without a hitch if it weren't for one man named Richard Deacon, who had served in the Canadian expedi-tionary force that marched on Red River in 1870. The angry man began heckling Riel halfway through his address.

"Criminal!" Deacon roared from the floor. "This man is a crim-inal and all he speaks are lies. We should have hanged him in 1870!"

Deacon was quickly ejected from the hall by those in the crowd who wanted to hear what the "criminal" had to say, and the lone dis-senting voice was quickly disregarded as that of an isolated extrem-ist. If only the Métis could have known that this one extremist was actually echoing the sentiments of the Ontario population. Riel fin-ished his speech, stressing unity and nonviolence.

"All of our communities must come together peaceably in our demand for responsible government. If our needs in the North-West can't be understood in Ottawa, then let them bend an ear to us. Let them hear our concerns and act upon them. This is all we want. This is all I'm here to accomplish." His moderation was welcomed with cheers and applause. Louis was in his element once again, basking in the glow of the political spotlight; he looked over to Gabriel Dumont and produced a wide smile.

The French-speaking Métis, the English-speaking settlers and Half-breeds in the region agreed to combine forces to form a central committee. The committee was to oversee the drafting of a petition of grievances to send to Ottawa. Louis Riel and William Henry Jackson of the Farmer's Union were the principal members of the committee, working long hours through the summer and into the fall to consult with all concerned parties and come up with a document that might fairly voice the sum of their grievances. There was grumbling from some quarters that they moved too slowly, but they wanted to be thorough. Louis also had to endure grumbling from his wife, who reminded him of his promise that they would be back in Montana by September.

"Just give me a little bit more time, Marguerite," was Louis' emphatic reply. "We are almost done here."

On December 16, the combined English-French committee finally endorsed and dispatched their petition to Secretary of State Joseph-Adolphe Chapleau in Ottawa. They had succeeded in presenting the concerns of all parties. The petition called for a responsible government locally, replacing the Ottawa-appointed North-West Council, and nationally, through fair representation by locally elected Members of Parliament. This issue had brought the disenfranchised French- and English-speakers together, but so did the question of land ownership. In recognition of Métis Native title, the petition called for a grant of land to Dumont and his people, while demanding that the current holdings be recognized in law. The petition also called upon Ottawa to live up to the treaty promises it had made to the Natives.

Here lay a sadly contentious issue. The Natives were ill-treated by the government, which may have been living up to the letter, though certainly not to the spirit, of its treaties with the Native tribes. Patronizingly and grudgingly, the Indian agents (men appointed by Ottawa to oversee the treaties who seemed to be selected by the virulence of their racism towards the Natives) doled out as little aid as they possibly could. The timing of their demands could not have been worse, as the Native cultures were faced with a veritable catas-trophe since the buffalo upon which they had depended for food, clothing and shelter for centuries had practically become extinct.

Starvation was rampant. Anger was widespread, and the Native tribes, prompted by the return of Riel, had also begun agitating for attention to their plight from Ottawa. Various chiefs gathered in mid-summer near Fort Carlton to discuss their grievances. The Cree chief Big Bear, who had yet to be pigeonholed onto a reserve by Ottawa despite constant pressure, was a lightning rod of discontent.

"I have been trying to seize the promises which they made to me," he addressed his fellow chiefs. "I have been grasping but I can-not find them. What they have promised me straightaway," he said of the government agents, "I have not yet seen the half of it. We have all been deceived in the same way."

His words certainly struck a chord with all present.

"I feel sad to abandon the liberty of my own land when they come to me and offer me small plots to stay on a reservation," Big Bear said in defense of his continued resistance to signing a gov-ernment treaty. "Especially when my people do not get half of what had been promised them in return."

Riel spoke with assembled Native chiefs in August 1884, remind-ing them that, just like their Métis cousins, they also had certain rights and that he had no qualms about voicing the Native concerns in his petition.

For the white settlers, this kind of talk and action was unsettling. Few homesteaders were enthusiastic about any sort of association with the "savage" Native hordes. The fact that Riel and the Métis were involved in these Native gatherings was enough to create a fis-sure in the whites' support for the brewing petition. Editorials in the local English papers shifted to a much more critical tone of Riel and Jackson's efforts.

The French-speaking Métis viewed matters far differently. Kin to the Native tribes, most especially the Cree, they were far more sympathetic. Dumont especially felt a strong bond with the region's indigenous populations.

"They are our relatives," Dumont explained to a visitor in the fall of 1884, "and when they are starving they come to us for relief, and we have to feed them. The government is not doing right by them."

Thus, in the end, despite the friction and loss of support it caused among their non-native allies, Riel and the Métis maintained modest demands on behalf of the Natives in the petition. And despite obstacles and delays, Riel saw his plan to appeal to Ottawa realized.

Now they had little to do but wait. No one would have dared to guess for how long. Secretary of State Chapleau acknowledged his receipt of the petition promptly. But this made the nearly two months' of waiting for further word from Ottawa even worse. Waiting through the very heart of winter, too, where there was little to distract the anxious Métis from dwelling on Ottawa's response to their requests.

The simmering tension began to have its effect on the Métis. As the more militant voices among Dumont's followers began to speak their discontent in louder voices, rumors began to spread that they were stockpiling weapons. And as frustration mounted, angry suggestions about taking a harder stand gained currency. The winter dragged by week after tortuous week, and as Riel's own anger began to boil over, he found himself growing ever more sympathetic to ideas of radical action. Gabriel Dumont had already made it known to his friend that he believed the petition had failed.

"The petition has accomplished nothing," he said to Riel. "Our words are lost on the government. Ottawa is swimming in words; all they have are words. What good will a few more words do to our people? The time for words is over; the time for action is now."

Then, on February 8, 1885, whatever fading hope the Métis still may have nurtured for a meaningful response from Ottawa was snuffed out altogether. A telegram forwarded to Charles Nolin by Lieutenant-Governor Edgar Dewdney, bypassing the acknowledged Métis leader Riel as a deliberate slight, met none of the petition's demands and addressed none of their grievances. It briefly and vaguely mused on the idea of establishing a further committee to complete a census of the North-West and investigate the petition's claims. For the Métis, Dewdney's response was a dismissive slap in the face. Ottawa had responded to their many concrete requests with ambiguous generalities.

Riel was having dinner with his family when a messenger told him about the government's reply. His face twisted into a look of such rage that his wife blanched and his children began to cry.

He slammed his fist on the table in anger and roared, "In 40 days, Ottawa will have my answer!"

Dumont arrived at Nolin's house a few hours later. Louis could tell by the look on his face that he was resolved to action.

"Words did not work," the big man said blankly. "Now we will try my way."

Riel nodded gravely before Gabriel wheeled about and stormed out of the house.

On March 1, Riel stood on the steps of the small St. Laurent de Grandin Church to address an angry congregation. Everyone could tell from the look on his face that this wasn't the same man who had urged a peaceful consensus a few months before.

"By now, you have all heard the government's response to our petition." There were agitated murmurs. "Like all of you, Gabriel Dumont and I do not believe that Ottawa has responded fairly. Either they do not think that we are serious or think so little of us that they think our concerns our irrelevant."

One or two men interrupted Louis with shouted insults at the prime minister.

"Let me assure you all that we do not intend to be trifled with, and that if Ottawa will not listen to reason, perhaps it is time the Métis bared their teeth."

It was then, amid the roars of the congregation's approval, that the spirit of the North-West Rebellion was born.

Yet, unlike the Red River Resistance, this time Louis would not have the backing of the Church. The split between the religious man and his religion began soon after Louis arrived in the summer of 1884. Father Alexis André was the most influential priest in the area, a man of deeply conservative inclination who believed deference to authority was among the greatest virtues. A staunch supporter of John A. Macdonald's Tories, the steely old priest had little respect for Louis Riel and his riotous history. He felt nothing but trepidation when word got out that the former Red River leader had come to the area. Hoping that the whole matter might resolve itself quietly, the Church remained noncommittal to the Métis movement through 1884 and the first months of 1885.

The Church's waffling did not sit well with the Métis, and when Bishop Vital Grandin from St. Albert, north of Fort Edmonton, visited in September 1884, Riel and Dumont let him know it. Most of their criticisms were leveled against Father André.

"The good Father hasn't been to a single one of our community meetings," Dumont said. "We have tried more than once to ask for his spiritual guidance, but he remains silent. From the beginning, my Métis have always been faithful to the Church, yet now that we need it most, it turns its back on us."

"It is the Métis' rebelliousness, your seeming eagerness to flout authority, that worries us," Grandin replied as gently as he could.

That was when Louis spoke up. "Tell me, my Reverend Father, since when have our priests become so preoccupied with obedience that they are blind to injustice?"

By the time Grandin left, it had become obvious to the Métis leaders that the Church wouldn't back them in their struggle against Ottawa. Nevertheless, the Métis community in the Saskatchewan valley stayed true to Riel and Dumont, even though the schism with the Church must have hurt the religious people deeply. Father André, bitter at the political movement that spread across his parish, developed a deep dislike for Louis Riel.

If Riel had become increasingly uneasy about his relationship with the Church throughout 1884, on March 15, 1885, he would sever all ties with the Catholic authority. It was now well known that the Métis had been stockpiling weapons and that most men in the community were preparing themselves for the worst. During Mass that day, Father Vital Fourmond made one last effort to avert the impending violence. Replacing the traditional Sunday sermon with a stern lecture on the sin of resistance to authority, Fourmond then announced that he would withhold the sacraments from anyone who joined the resistance against Ottawa. None of the parishioners could believe their ears, least of all Louis Riel, who was sitting at the back of the Church.

"What is this?" Louis yelled as he leapt to his feet. "Is the Church now preaching the words of Ottawa? If it is, Father, let me warn you that the words that come from that city cannot be counted on. I can personally guarantee you that."

"Louis Riel!" Fourmond roared with the godliest voice he could muster. "How dare you interrupt God's service!"

"This is not God's service," Louis responded evenly. "It is the prime minister's."

The congregation gasped in shock as Riel turned and walked out of the church. One by one, the rest of the Métis followed him out, until Fourmond found himself standing in front of rows of empty pews.

Lawrence Clarke, the chief factor of the Hudson's Bay Company in nearby Fort Carlton, provided the final push to armed rebellion. In response to the rising tensions in the Saskatchewan valley, Lieutenant-Governor Dewdney decided that he would try to frighten the Métis into subservience. He sent Clarke a telegram, instructing the factor to inform the local Métis that Canada was sending a military contingent to return peace to the region. No such force was in existence yet, but Dewdney hoped that mention of such a force would take the fire out of the Métis. Clarke enthusiastically complied.

He ran into a group of Métis men on March 17 and quickly got to work. "Ho there!" he called out to the men. "Have you heard any answer from Ottawa about your lands?" The tone of Clarke's voice was outright condescension.

One of the Métis shrugged and said that they had not.

"I didn't think so," he scoffed. "In fact, I'm sure that the only answer you're going to get will be bullets."

This got the men's attention.

"What do you mean by that?" one of the men snapped.

"I mean that word is there's near 100 armed soldiers headed from Regina to Prince Albert as we speak. I've heard that they aim to arrest Gabriel Dumont and Louis Riel."

The news was false and meant to frighten the Métis into abandoning their cause, but it only served to incite them. The men galloped into Batoche, and word of the approaching soldiers spread like wildfire from one Métis community to another. The next day a throng of armed Métis men crowded around the Church of St. Antoine de Padoue in Batoche, waiting for Dumont and Riel to show up. A priest named Julien Moulin stood atop the church's main stairs, trying to get the men to disperse. None of the assembled men were listening.

Riel and Dumont arrived together in mid-afternoon amid a great collective cheer. Parting the crowd, the two leaders walked up the steps to where Father Moulin was still standing.

"It is important that we have a meeting immediately, Father," Louis said. "We need to use the Church."

"The House of God will not be sullied by your political wrangling," Moulin replied.

Louis stared at the priest for an instant before deciding he had taken enough from the Saskatchewan clergy.

"Get out of my way!" he yelled at Moulin as he grabbed the priest by the shoulder. "Rome has fallen!"

Riel then tossed Moulin into the crowd below. "Take him away! I never want to see the face of this pretender again!"

Once they were settled inside, Dumont was the first to speak, his rumbling voice spilling over the pews full of armed men. "The police are coming to take Louis Riel. They call him a criminal. His crime? Standing up for our people."

Gabriel walked across the front of the church and put his hand on Louis' shoulder. "Just as he worked for Red River against Ottawa so many years ago, so too has he worked tirelessly for us. But this time we cannot let him be pushed into exile. This time we must make a stand for him!"

The men cheered their agreement in unison, filling the church with their shouts.

Louis stepped forward, and the church instantly grew quiet. "Gabriel, I thank you, as I thank all of you, my brothers," Riel said, his voice choked with emotion. "I know how this works. I've been here before. We send petitions, they send soldiers to take us— Gabriel and me. In their eyes, it is I who have done wrong. The government hates me because I already made them give in once. This time they will give up nothing." Louis paused, his eyes going from the gathered men to where Dumont was standing.

"I say to you now," Louis continued, "that I think it would be better for me to go. I must leave you, and I feel I should go now. Once I am gone you may get what you want more easily." A few men in the pews started shouting their objections, but Louis spoke over them. "Yes, I really think it would be better if I went back to Montana."

The whole crowd offered their resounding rejection to Louis' idea. The church became a cacophony of disagreement.

Gabriel Dumont stepped forward again. "I say Louis Riel stays, and we fight! All in favor of taking up arms, raise your hand!"

All the men in the church rose in unison, holding their rifles and revolvers aloft. The Métis were going to war.

CHAPTER TEN

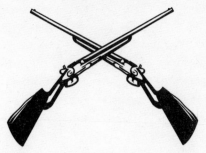

Rebellion

THE CANADIAN AUTHORITIES were not caught off guard by the Métis rebellion. Major Leif Crozier, commanding officer of the North-West Mounted Police in Prince Albert, had a thorough network of spies reporting to him from around the Saskatchewan valley, and he knew all too well how frustrated the Métis were growing with Ottawa. In early March, he mustered a militia of 50 Prince Albert volunteers who were to accompany his 50 Mounties to Fort Carlton. Crozier was certain that if the Métis did resort to armed rebellion, their first move would be to occupy the Hudson's Bay Company's trading post, and he wasted no time fortifying it. He and his troop of 100 men arrived at Fort Carlton on March 13.

The whole countryside was buzzing with talk of rebellion by the time Crozier got to the trading post on the North Saskatchewan, and he promptly telegraphed Lieutenant-Governor Dewdney.

His terse message sent tremors all the way to Ottawa: "Half-breed rebellion likely to break out any moment. Must be prepared for consequences. Troop must be largely reinforced. French Half-breeds alone in this section number 700 men. If Half-breed rise, Indians will join them."

Leif Crozier (1847–1901), NWMP Superintendent of Fort Carlton in 1880, five years before the battle at Duck Lake

With the specter of a full-scale Native war looming over Ottawa, Prime Minister Macdonald (who had regained power in 1878) called up the Canadian militia on March 23, placing Major-General Frederick D. Middleton in command. Indeed, to the Saskatchewan Métis, it might have seemed as if every Canadian man with a rifle was coming west to set things straight. Even as preparations began for the deployment of Middleton's force from Ontario, Colonel

Acheson Gosford Irvine of the North-West Mounted Police was ordered to march 100 Mounties from Regina to Prince Albert. Back in Fort Carlton, Crozier knew full well that it was only a matter of time before reinforcements would arrive and aimed to stay put until his position was strengthened.

That was his intention, anyway, but the men under his command had different ideas. Almost every fighting man in Fort Carlton held the Métis in the lowest esteem, and the general opinion among the troops was that the uprising would be over and done with the moment their column appeared marching towards Batoche. The men of the Prince Albert militia were especially eager to voice their military opinions, and as each day of waiting dragged on, Crozier found himself coming under more and more pressure to act.

He was not alone. In the Métis camp, Louis Riel was being urged daily by Gabriel Dumont to take the fight to the approaching Canadians. Yet even as Canadian soldiers were mobilizing against his movement, Riel was doing all he could to avoid violence. Holding out for the hope that Ottawa would send diplomatic negotiators, Louis ordered Dumont and his warriors to stand down.

"But Louis," Dumont said, "they have many more men, arms and ammunition than we do. We will never win on the open battlefield. We have to fight them in the darkness, raid their supplies, strike terror into their hearts."

"Never!" came Louis' stern rebuke. "We will not fight like the savages they believe us to be. If we were fighting a war of extermination, we could put every farm from here to Regina to the torch and bring the sword upon women and children. But no, we are God's soldiers, and we will only strike when we are set upon. This is my word. This is the will of God."

It says much of Louis' influence over Gabriel that the hardheaded Métis warrior, girded for battle and convinced his guerrilla tactics would win the day, took Riel's preaching to heart and kept his equally eager Métis fighters from attacking. Indeed, Louis had come to occupy such a lofty position among the Métis that if he wasn't quite looked upon as a saint, he was at least a divine messenger. Louis did nothing to discourage such musings. In fact, his new system of government actively encouraged it.

Riel preached that Métis success would depend on their purity and obedience to the Lord's word. To this end, Riel established a governing council called the Exovedate, made up a number of appointed officials called Exovedes, meaning "out of the flock" in Latin. The Exovedate, and the issues it debated, revealed the extent to which Riel had slipped into his convoluted spiritual vision. While the Exovedate presided over the minutiae of daily life—dispensing free passes for the local ferries and even judging the ownership of individual, stray cows—its primary focus was to remake the world from the ground up.

As Gabriel Dumont and his soldiers were plotting ways to repel the imminent Canadian attack, Riel's Exovedate was busy tackling abstract religious questions. Seizing the opportunity to enact the tenets of his theology that had begun in his exile and insanity, Riel declared that the Catholic Sabbath would be changed from Sunday to Saturday and that his old confidant, Bishop Bourget, was to be formally recognized as the first "Pope of the New World." The council of Exovedes took the final step when they passed a resolution recognizing "Louis David Riel as a prophet in the service of Jesus Christ and Son of God and only Redeemer of the world." Finally, after all his years of inner doubt and exile, Louis Riel had achieved divinity—at the price, many would say of his sanity.

Of course, none of these religious pronouncements proved useful to the Métis in the face of the approaching Canadians, who did not seem so concerned about the Métis standing with God. While Louis was busy making Batoche into a fortress of God, both militarily and morally, Gabriel Dumont was trying to figure out how the Métis, short on ammunition and weapons, would stand a fighting chance on any battlefield against the better-equipped Canadian forces. It was a difficult position for the pragmatic man, who endlessly pitted the strategic reality of the Métis situation with a desperate wish to believe in Riel's self-appointed divinity. More often than not, he gave in to Louis' orders, but when he decided to act, no amount of sermonizing would stop him.

The first occasion came when word reached Batoche that the NWMP were using Duck Lake as a reconnaissance base. Situated just a few miles from Batoche on the other side of the South Saskatchewan River, Duck Lake was a little bit too close for comfort, even for Louis Riel. So Dumont got the Métis leader's blessing to lead a hand-picked cadre of 10 Métis fighters out to Duck Lake to investigate the situation. It was late March by this time, and Dumont, having spent the last few weeks twitching under Riel's sit-and-wait game, was itching for action. He would end up doing much more than investigating.

On the evening of March 24, Dumont and his men were scouting the area when they ran into a party of 15 Mounties who were doing the same. The night was pitch black, and the two groups of mounted men practically ran into each other.

"Hold!" Dumont roared, uncertain about how many men he was confronting in the darkness. "This is Métis land! Who are you, and what are you doing here!"

The voice that responded was not nearly so firm. "We are a party of North-West Mounted Police patrolling the Queen's land."

Somebody lit a lantern, and Gabriel could dimly make out the man who addressed him. It was a young Mountie who looked to be little more than 20 years old, uncertain and obviously afraid in his starched uniform. Dumont did not feel a single spark of sympathy for his enemy.

Spurring his horse forward a few paces, Dumont reached out and grabbed the reins of the youngster's horse. "I'm afraid you've taken a wrong turn," Dumont barked at the Mountie. "You are now a prisoner of the Métis."

The Mountie reacted, lunging for the revolver at his side, but Dumont was too quick, and delivered a backhanded fist across the young man's face before he could pull his gun. Dazed and bleeding heavily from the mouth and nose, the police officer barely managed to hold on to his mount. That was when the nearest Mountie went for his gun as well, but he wasn't quick enough either. Before he was even able to haul his gun from its holster, Gabriel unslung his rifle from around his shoulders, cocked the lever and had it aimed straight at the second officer's head. An instant later the rest of the Métis and the Mounties drew their guns and cocked them. For a second or two, the darkness came to life with the metallic sound of firearms being put to the ready, followed by a long silence bloated with a sense of impending violence. The only men without firearms in their hands were the two in front of Gabriel: the bleeding youngster still too dazed to know what was going on and the other frozen in fear at the wrong end of Dumont's Winchester.

Several tense moments passed before Dumont broke the silence. "Get out of here, you dogs!" He roared at the top of his voice. "Go back and tell your masters that you were too frightened to face down a handful of Métis!"

The Mounties didn't need to be told twice. Dumont hadn't finished his insult when all of them turned and galloped away as a single body, heading back north to Fort Carlton. The Métis shouted cheers and taunts at their backs, while Gabriel beamed with glee. Finally, he was fighting the Canadians on his own terms.

Word of the humiliating standoff reached Fort Carlton ahead of the retreating Mounties, and it caused quite a stir. Crozier had been having problems keeping his garrison within the fort walls, so eager were his men to take on the Métis. Until March 23, Crozier had been able to stave off criticism of his cautious strategy, arguing that Colonel Irvine and his 100 Mounties were expected to arrive at the fort any day. But Dumont's modest victory against the NWMP scouts aggravated the Canadians, and Crozier found himself under immense pressure to respond to the Métis' belligerence. He would eventually be goaded into acting.

"Are we to be turned back by a parcel of Half-breeds?" asked Hudson's Bay factor Lawrence Clarke, when Crozier expressed doubts about retaliating. "Now is the time, Crozier," Clarke continued. "The men are starting to call you a bloody coward."

That they were. Nearly all the Prince Albert men were eager to prove their mettle against what they believed to be a mere "parcel of Half-breeds," and could not understand their commanding officer's hesitation. For his part, Crozier had managed to stave off his soldiers' thirst for bloodshed through much of March, but when his courage was called into question, the Mountie officer promptly caved to the pressure and ordered his force to march south. His force soon met up with the smaller group of police who were retreating from their humbling at the hands of Dumont, and these men joined the expedition south. On the morning of March 26, a total of 56 North-West Mounted Police, 43 volunteers and teamsters and a venerable 7-pound cannon descended on Duck Lake.

Métis scouts quickly sent word back to Batoche: "The police are coming!"

Word spread quickly through the Métis communities, leaving a frenetic urgency in their wake. Women fell to their knees and prayed for fathers, husbands and sons, who armed themselves, said their farewells and left for battle. Dumont and his men had only just returned from their earlier standoff with the Mounties when they heard of Crozier's approach, and they wasted no time clambering astride their steeds again and plowing through the crisp spring snow towards an uncertain fate.

Gabriel rounded up every Métis soldier he could find on his way north. Riel, convinced that Crozier's troop was an aggressive force, also led a contingent of Métis soldiers out of Batoche. Resolved to battle, Louis Riel wore a grave expression as he rode at the head of the Métis column. With Riel carrying an enormous bronze crucifix in both hands and staring solemnly ahead, the Batoche men looked like an armed and mounted parish procession. By the time all the men converged on Duck Lake, they numbered over 200. Most of them were Métis, but a good number of Cree and Sioux also stood next to their Plains brethren.

The tactician in Gabriel immediately set to work. He marched the force about two miles from Duck Lake and had them take defensive positions in a low, bushy depression near the Carlton Trail, the road that Crozier likely would be marching down. He was right. A short time later, Crozier's force appeared. Informed of the Métis presence by Mountie scouts, the troops drew to a halt just within rifle range. Major Crozier ordered the force's sleds arranged across the trail to form a defensive wall, and he had a group of Mounties bring the cannon to the front. All the while, the Métis riflemen crept along the ground towards Crozier's force, staying close to the ground and finding cover in the thick bush near the trail and behind a nearby cabin. They soon formed a semi-circle around Crozier's men. The battle lines were drawn.

Dumont and Riel sent forth Gabriel's brother, Isidore, and an old Cree Native named Asiyiwin. The pair walked towards Crozier's men under a white flag of truce, hoping to parley. Crozier himself straightened his NWMP tunic, adjusted his cap and road out to meet Isidore and Asiyiwin along with an English Half-breed named Joe McKay who was to serve as an interpreter.

"What do you want?" Crozier asked Isidore, refusing to even acknowledge the elder Cree standing next to Gabriel's brother.

Isidore was about to respond when Asiyiwin took matters into his own hands. The old Cree, seemingly oblivious to the tension hanging thick in the air, took exception to the fact that Joe McKay was so heavily armed, with two pistols jutting out of his gun belt and a rifle and shotgun strapped to his saddle.

"Where are you going with all those guns, grandson?" Asiyiwin asked just before he reached forward and tried to grab one of McKay's revolvers from his belt.

A struggle ensued as McKay grabbed Asiyiwin by the wrist and tried to yank the old man off his horse. Isidore, uncertain of what to do, moved for his own rifle. Before Isidore was able to draw his weapon, McKay got the better of his much elder opponent, pulling one of his pistols and firing at Asiyiwin at point-blank range. The

Native toppled from his mount, dead. That was when Crozier decided he'd had enough. Wheeling his horse away from the scene, Crozier galloped back towards the line of sleds. Isidore was just turning around to head back to his side when Crozier gave the order to fire. Louis, Gabriel and the rest of Métis watched in horror as Isidore was gunned down in the snow.

In the next instant, both sides opened fire, the Métis from within the cover of the surrounding bush, the Canadians from behind their sleds. Among all the combatants, only Louis Riel seemed unconcerned with the shooting. Leaping up onto his horse he held his enormous crucifix aloft as he galloped up and down the Métis line.

"In the name of God who created us, answer their fire!" he roared above the cacophony of battle.

"*Tabernac!*" Dumont yelled at Louis when he rode by him. "Get off your horse or you'll be killed!"

But much to the awe of all, Louis paid no attention to his friend's warning and continued to ride in the open among his followers, shouting encouragement and calling down the blessing of God. Maybe it was his prayers, the superior marksmanship of the Métis, superior numbers or better cover, but whatever the case, it wasn't long before the battle began to turn decidedly in favor of the Métis. While the Mounties' cannon jammed after only two shots, the riflemen in the bush were picking off their outflanked foes, who were clinging to the poor cover of their sleighs. An improvised charge by a group of Prince Albert volunteers was quickly stopped when the Métis' gunfire promptly cut down every man who charged across the open plain.

Dumont sensed impending victory and whooped for joy at the sight of the hemmed-in Canadians. Running from bush to bush, Dumont was raining deadly accurate fire on Crozier's force when a single Mountie bullet grazed his skull. Gabriel toppled into the snow, knocked unconscious by the force of the blow, and for a moment, many of the Métis believed they had lost two Dumont brothers that day.

But the redoubtable hunter stayed down for only a moment. Pressing his hand against his heavily bleeding head, he rose to one knee and waved at his troops, signaling that he was all right. Still, the injury was enough to take the fight out of Dumont for the day. The Canadians had had enough as well.

Whittled down from 100 to less than 80 men in all of about 20 minutes of fighting, Crozier's force somehow managed to back out of the lethal trap. They left the bloodstained field littered with many of their dead and wounded, beating a hasty retreat with every casualty they were able to carry. The Canadians were in full flight, and an enraged Edouard Dumont, the third Dumont brother, rallied the riflemen.

"After them!" he roared at his confederates. "Destroy them all!"

The battle might have ended in complete slaughter if Riel had not galloped to the front of the firing line.

"No!" he yelled back at the men. "Let them go. We have seen enough bloodshed today."

Thus, Crozier's expedition was spared only by Louis Riel's magnanimity. With 12 men killed and 11 wounded, Crozier limped back to Fort Carlton. If it were up to him, Dumont wouldn't have let the Canadians get away. The big fighter was up on his feet soon after his head wound was bandaged, and still reeling from the death of his brother, he was putting together a force that would deal the death-blow to the retreating force. Again, Riel intervened.

"No, Gabriel," he said gently, resting a hand on Dumont's shoulder. "We will let the men be. Let us instead tend to the wounded they have left in the field." Gabriel began to protest, but Louis interrupted. "During the battle, we are warriors, but after the fighting is over, let us again be Christians."

The Métis headed back to Batoche carrying the exuberance of victory high on their shoulders. Having lost only five men of 200 in the fighting at Duck Lake, there was good reason for celebration. News of the battle spread across the prairie, and for a short time at

Cree chiefs Big Bear (*left,* 1825–88) and Poundmaker (1842–86) in 1886 while they were incarcerated for their part in the North-West Rebellion. Although it is widely believed that both men urged peace for their respective bands, many of the warriors under them were eager to join the Métis. Big Bear's Cree killed settlers in Frog Lake and razed Fort Pitt, while the Cree from Poundmaker's reserve took Battleford. In the end, both men's forces were defeated. Poundmaker's warriors lost out at the battle of Cut Knife Hill when they faced a force of 325 militia under Lieutenant-Colonel William Otter. Big Bear's braves were likewise defeated when they fought a Canadian force under the command of Major-General T.B. Strange at Frenchman's Butte.

least, the Métis movement gathered momentum, threatening to spark the widespread discontent of the Plains Natives into full-scale rebellion. Over the next few days, groups of Native warriors arrived from different tribes around the South Saskatchewan to join Riel and Dumont's rebels. On March 30, Cree chief Poundmaker launched his own offensive, sacking the town of Battleford on the North Saskatchewan River. On April 2, a group of Cree under Chief Big Bear killed nine Canadians to the north near Frog Lake.

As promising as the Cree cooperation was, Duck Lake turned out to be the rebellion's high tide. For even while Chief Crowfoot ordered his mighty Blackfoot Confederacy to remain neutral in the fight against Ottawa, General Middleton's military juggernaut was heading into the region. His enormous force in Qu'Appelle had grown to over 2000 men by early April. Devising a three-pronged strategy to thwart the rebellion, Middleton decided to divide his army, ordering Lieutenant-Colonel William Otter to engage Poundmaker in Battleford; sending another senior officer, Major-General Thomas Bland Strange, after Big Bear in the north; and personally command-ing the force that would march to Batoche to meet Riel's Métis.

So it was that Middleton's force left Qu'Appelle on a cold April 6 morning—more than 800 soldiers armed with the best weapons of the day and 120 vehicles loaded with supplies and ammunition. The force slowly and deliberately made its way north to Batoche, and with every step, the anxiety in Batoche increased. Riel and Dumont were facing the same old problem. Riel, still flushed from the victory at Duck Lake, insisted that the Métis stay close to Batoche, while Dumont believed victory was possible only if they engaged the enemy in guerrilla warfare—attacking behind enemy lines, con-ducting raids for desperately needed ammunition and harrying the largely green soldiers every step of the way. Yet, if Riel was adamant about maintaining the moral high ground before, the Battle of Duck Lake only cemented the idea in his head.

Convinced that they had won the day against Crozier because God had weighed in on their side, Riel argued tirelessly that the

Major-General Frederick D. Middleton (1825–98), commander of
the force sent out to put down the North-West Rebellion

Métis should remain upright. His reasons were hardly coherent, and
while Dumont was frustrated, he also found himself daring to
believe.

"Let us not slink through the darkness like so many serpents,
stabbing at their backs when they cannot see us," Riel would say.
"No, let us stand proudly in front of them under the daylight, soldiers of God, who look their enemy in the face."

And so, in accordance with Riel's wishes, Middleton encountered next to no resistance as he traveled north. Just as before, Gabriel Dumont's faith in Riel's vision began to wane as Middleton's men grew closer. Not to challenge the enormous force even once as it made its way towards them flew in the face all Dumont's military instincts. He continued to nag Riel, until finally, in mid-April, Riel gave his exasperated permission to move against the approaching soldiers. By this time, Middleton's men were less than two days' march away from Batoche.

Dumont, Riel and 230 Métis, Sioux and Cree set out from Batoche on the evening of April 23. Their destination was Tourond's Coulee, a deep ravine that flanked Fish Creek, where Dumont planned to lay his ambush against Middleton's soldiers as they made their way down a nearby trail. On the first night's march, an incoming scout informed the Métis of a rumor that another Mountie force was spotted leaving Qu'Appelle, possibly heading for Batoche. Upon hearing this, many of the men in the party wanted to go back and defend their homes. Dumont convinced them that 50 men should be sufficient, and ordered this contingent to head back with Louis Riel at their head. Dumont actually breathed a sigh of relief after Riel departed.

"Thank God he's going back," he was heard muttering to himself, "we'll be able to move faster now that we aren't praying so much."

Some of the more irreverent chuckled at Dumont's comment. It was true that Riel had made the entire Métis column stop half a dozen times to join in group prayer. Dumont's men arrived at Tourond's Coulee in the small hours of April 24. They wasted no time laying their ambush in the densely wooded ravine along Fish Creek

The strategy was to remain concealed in the ravine until Middleton's force passed by on the adjacent road. Only when they passed would the Métis soldiers climb up from the ravine and fire on their rear from the cover of the trees. If they could have executed the plan, it would have been devastating. With nearly 200 Métis rifles opening up on the back of the column, it is easy to imagine the kind of destruction this would have unleashed. But fate was conspiring against Dumont's men.

As the sun's first rays rose on the morning of the April 24, 1885, Middleton's advance scouts noticed the churned-up trail cresting the coulee. The sheer number of tracks on the road gave away Dumont's hidden men, and a short reconnoiter into the ravine revealed the presence of waiting Métis. As the two scouts galloped back to Middleton, Dumont cursed the clumsiness of his men. He had warned them repeatedly to stay clear of the road throughout the night for precisely this reason. Now they could only wait as Middleton's force approached. They wouldn't have to wait long.

The first casualty at the Battle of Fish Creek was a Sioux warrior in full war paint who charged up to the lip of the ravine and made a headlong dash towards the approaching enemy, sending his lone war cry into the prairie wind. Middleton's men riddled the solitary man with bullets before continuing on to the ravine.

Confused skirmishing between the two forces—the Métis well covered in the bottom of the ravine, the Canadian soldiers firing down from their exposed positions above—turned into a full-fledged battle that raged throughout the morning. While Métis casualties were light, they suffered mostly from desertion. The sheer firepower of the Canadians at the top of the ravine was enough to impel many of Dumont's men to think twice about the rebellion. As ineffectual as most of the Canadians' firing was, the sheer volume of lead that filled the bottom of Tourond's Coulee was nothing short of staggering. Middleton's men had even managed to set up a nine-pounder cannon at the edge of the ravine. Nevertheless, those who tried to man it became exposed to the Métis sharpshooters below, and the Canadians took severe casualties trying to fire artillery into the Métis gulch.

Although Dumont's position was tenable, the Métis were deserting in droves, and by midday, he was down to a mere 54 fighters. Meanwhile, the Métis in Batoche could hear the distant cannon reverberating ominously through the land. Riel, shaken by the

The Battle of Fish Creek raged all day on April 24. Muzzle flashes of the Métis riflemen are visible in the lower right corner.

sounds of fighting, decided to pray. Falling on his knees, he appealed to God on behalf of the Métis soldiers. He extended his arms on either side of him as if he were being crucified on an imaginary cross; he stayed in the position for such a long time that he had the women and children in town take turns holding up his arms so that they would not waver. Gabriel's brother, Edouard, found little comfort in Riel's religious ardor. As each hour wore on, he grew increasingly restless, worrying about the fate of the men in the coulee—about his brother. Finally, unable to take the waiting anymore, Edouard approached Louis, who was still kneeling, arms outstretched, in the center of town. Edouard stared at his leader incredulously.

"We need to go help Gabriel," he said to Louis.

"Don't worry," Riel assured him with mystical certainty, "they are under my watch. No harm will come to them."

Edouard lost his patience. "It is your word against the sound of cannon and rifle. Do you mean to tell me that God can stop a bullet? Then why did he allow dozens of them to strike down Isidore?"

Louis only stared blankly, his arms still outstretched, concentrating intently on something else that Edouard could not see.

"My people are in peril," Edouard continued, "and I cannot remain here and hope for the best. I cannot remain here and let them be killed without going to their aid."

He quickly gathered all 80 fighting men at Batoche to him and galloped off to help his brother, leaving Riel alone with the women and children.

Dumont and his core group of men were still fighting in the coulee when Edouard and the others arrived. Shortly after Gabriel's numbers were bolstered by his brother's arrival, Middleton decided the Métis in the gulch were more trouble than they were worth. Content to let his enemies hold the ravine, Middleton pulled his soldiers back. He had taken more than enough casualties in an inconsequential fight for an unimportant piece of territory. The Battle of Fish Creek was over the same day it began, a failed ambush that resulted in four Métis dead and two wounded. The Canadians got the worst of things again, as the deadly Métis marksmanship took its toll, leaving 10 soldiers dead and 45 wounded.

Fish Creek was certainly not a decisive battle, but the Métis' fighting ability was dramatically reduced after the battle. Not only did Dumont lose huge numbers to desertion, but most of his troops' horses were killed during the exchange, and the protracted shooting left their ammunition stores at next to nothing. All he could do was order a march back to Batoche, where they would wait for Middleton's inevitable attack.

They did not wait idly. The Métis dug a system of rifle pits surrounding the town and sent out a last word for help, accepting any man who could fire a rifle. At the end of April, Dumont had about 160 Métis and Natives under his command—hardly encouraging numbers, considering that Middleton had also received reinforcements when Colonel Irvine joined his army with 150 Mounties, bringing the Canadian fighting force to roughly 950 men. Yet this wasn't even the worst of the news. The biggest problem that the Métis were facing was their severe shortage of ammunition. Down to almost no bullets, the riflemen scoured the countryside in their spare time, looking for anything they could find that could be fired from a rifle.

All the Métis present must have known the odds were bad, but they fought anyway. Under Dumont's direction, the Métis had prepared well, their skillfully constructed rifle pits providing them with an effective defensive position. As for ammunition, they had gathered a makeshift store of appropriately shaped rocks, nails and bullets fashioned from melted-down tin cans. Indeed, spirits were remarkably high as the ever-energetic Gabriel Dumont made his rounds through the rifle pits, encouraging each and every man with his bold presence.

Middleton's force licked its wounds from the Fish Creek encounter for about two weeks before resuming its inexorable advance towards Batoche. They arrived on May 9, initiating the battle that would last for the next four days. It would be Riel and Dumont's last stand against the Canadian government.

Middleton, originally dismissive of Métis fighting ability, had become markedly more cautious after the losses suffered at Fish Creek. He possessed an almost overwhelming superiority, both in numbers of men and in equipment, but his strategy in the battle around Batoche would be marked by an extremely tenuous strategy,

The first shots fired at the Battle of Batoche were fired along this fence in May 1885.

where his men inched their way forward at an excruciatingly slow pace, exchanging fire with the dug-in Métis. Canadian cannons and a Gatling gun pounded the Métis lines and homes in Batoche day after day. And still, Middleton sent forward only probing attacks. The pessimistic commanding officer was convinced that he lacked the manpower to take the town.

He wired the minister of defense in Ottawa: "Am in rather ticklish position. Force can succeed holding but no more—want more troops."

Obviously, he had no way of knowing how desperate the situation had become for the Métis, who were barely able to return fire anymore, so short were they on ammunition. A group of Canadian officers came to realize this, and completely fed up with their commander's temerity, secretly concocted a plan to charge the enemy lines on their own authority. On the morning of May 12, the fourth day of the battle, an ambitious lieutenant-colonel, Arthur Williams, assembled his troops.

He spoke to his soldiers in a voice barely above a whisper: "I have no orders to do what I am going to do, but I am confident that Batoche can be taken on this very day. I am taking ultimate responsibility for this decision, not General Middleton. I only ask that you follow me into the village. By God's grace, this Louis Riel will fall on our charge."

Colonel Williams cast one look at the grimy faces of the determined and fed-up men around him and knew that they would charge with him. They rushed the Métis positions later that day, and by sheer numbers, overwhelmed the thinly manned Métis lines, pushing Dumont's riflemen to their second row of rifle pits. That was when the fierce fighting began, as the Métis, led by Gabriel, ran from trench to trench, firing as they fell back, contesting every yard of prairie they gave up. Finally, however, there were no more rifle pits to which they could run and no more ammunition that they could fire.

The Canadians gunned down the trapped Métis like fish in a barrel, and this was when most of their casualties in the battle occurred. Gabriel Dumont was in one of the last rifle pits to fall, standing shoulder to shoulder with a 93-year-old Métis by the name of Joseph Oullette, emptying his last rounds into the ranks of the oncoming Canadian soldiers.

"C'mon old man," Gabriel finally bellowed over the din of the battle, "it's time to go."

"Wait just another minute," came Oullette's response, "I want to kill one more Englishman."

Depicting Riel's surrender, this illustration was drawn for *The Canadian Pictorial and Illustrated War News.*

These would be the old Oullette's last words. In the next moment, a group of Canadian soldiers flooded the rifle pit, brandishing their bayoneted rifles. Oullette was killed by a bayonet through the stomach, but the fierce Dumont, using his rifle as a club, smashed his way through the attackers and retreated to Batoche, making one more stand in the town before retreating farther into the surrounding forest. The Métis continued to put up a fierce, if desultory resistance for a few days, but the back of the Métis rebellion was broken. The Fortress of God had fallen.

Riel and his family were among the refugees hiding in the woods along the South Saskatchewan River. He ran into Dumont shortly after the fight.

"What are we going to do?" the Métis leader asked, suddenly unsure of himself, his mission and his vision. He looked at his general's expressionless face, smudged with blood and grime.

"What are we going to do?" he said again, this time more to himself than Dumont.

The death and defeat Dumont had witnessed in the preceding hours had stripped him of any tact he may have ever possessed.

"We must die," he told Riel flatly. "You must have known that in taking up arms against such a power we would be defeated."

But when he looked into Louis' devastated eyes, he suddenly realized that the leader of the rebellion really did believe that God was looking after them. In the end, there was some small part of Louis that had expected a miracle. And now, after all the death and difficulty, he was struggling with the realization that he was no prophet of God, only a scared man hiding in the woods, an outlaw once again.

It was the last time that Riel was ever to see Gabriel Dumont. Dumont spent the next several days evading Canadian patrols and planning his escape south of the border. Middleton had extended an offer of surrender to the two leaders. Riel, hoping that the anger of Canada might be focused on him and not his people, turned himself in. As Riel was interned in Middleton's camp, playing the role of the gentleman prisoner with the British major-general, the resourceful Dumont did his best to shrug off memories of his lost home, and he headed for the United States where he lived until amnesty was granted in 1888.

CHAPTER ELEVEN

Treason

THE COUNTRY HAD BEEN RIVETED by the drama of the rebellion, a drama that was only heightened when Riel's story became a trial. In the days before television, radio or cinema, the humble newspaper was the lone ruler of the public media. Wherever it shone its spotlight, the public gaze followed. The Riel trial became akin to the latest hit television drama, the blockbuster summer film and the best-selling crime novel all rolled into one. The nation, East and West, French and English, were hooked and snapped up copies of dailies to read the latest chapter in the dramatic saga.

This common interest, however, was the only way in which the country was united in regard to Louis Riel. The Métis leader embodied a series of overlapping, very Canadian, bipolarities. Encapsulated here was the story of the giant eastern political and financial power in its blundering conquest of the West. Indeed, Riel and the Métis were located at the juncture of conflicting cultures brought on by western expansion. Part Native, part European, the Métis themselves were a product of the collision between East and West in the Canadian hinterlands. But more than anything else, the ramifications *chis phe.*

of Riel's struggle polarized French and English public opinion into two opposing camps.

There is little doubt that political actors in Québec played upon the symbolism in Riel's persecution for their own purposes. Riel's trial was undeniably about more, or perhaps less, than a simple Protestant English desire to keep the French Catholics in their "proper place." After all, Riel did lead an armed rebellion against the legally constituted government of Canada. As well, he had, quite disturbingly from a Roman Catholic point of view, maintained heretical propositions regarding the Holy Mother Church.

Yet uncomfortable complications such as these were shunted aside as the politically ambitious rushed forward to wield Riel's perceived victimization as a national symbol. Moreover, what did prominent Québec ministers, complicit at the very least in Ottawa's neglect of Métis grievances, have to say for themselves? Indeed, what of Québec public opinion? Until this time, it had languished, largely uninterested, as tensions mounted in the West. It had even signed on for a military response to the rebellion, and a militia had been dispatched from Montréal.

On the other hand, there was some measure of truth in the French nationalists' accusation that the rebellion was largely a result of Orange Ontario's penchant for bullying French-Canadian Catholics into submission. The underlying current of distrust, even hatred, of French Catholicism promulgated by the scores of Orange Lodges across the country was as strong then as it is strange and repugnant today. Riel, for those of this bigoted ilk, was like a line in the sand: a threatening "papist" tendril that had to be chopped off before it gained too strong a hold in the West—a region that, according to this faction, was to be solidly Anglo-Saxon. Nor were the Orangemen exactly shy about expressing their views.

Given this, is it any wonder that Louis Riel became a symbolic line in the sand for French Canadians as well? The elite of Lower Canada had agreed to enter a larger Canadian Confederation in part because of what it understood as a partnership with the English to expand into the West, settling and developing it together. Subsequent events throughout the country had since exposed this ideal of equality between French and English as a cruel illusion; the treatment of Riel and the Métis was like a final unveiling.

So it was, that in the light of such underlying tensions, General Middleton decided to ship Riel to Winnipeg shortly after his capture. The only sizeable town in the prairies, it was a logical location for the Métis rebel's trial. Nevertheless, Minister of Justice Alexander Campbell wrote that he feared a miscarriage of justice if Riel was tried in Manitoba.

Accordingly, the militia minister had rushed a terse telegraph off to Middleton: "Minister of Justice for judicial reasons wishes prisoner sent to Regina and not to Winnipeg."

The telegram reached Middleton in time and Riel was diverted to Regina, although whether this last minute transfer averted a miscarriage of justice or was actually responsible for one is open to debate. By switching the trial site from Winnipeg to Regina, the Dominion government guaranteed that Riel would receive a hearing that was less fair. Manitoba, as a full-fledged province, was governed by the criminal judicial proceedings and laws as were the other provinces, but formal justice in Regina, which was located in the vast North-West Territories, was a very different beast altogether. Owing to the sparse settlement of the relatively small population, the Dominion government had enacted the North-West Territories Act of 1880, allowing for more economical judicial proceedings in the enormous region.

This meant profound differences for Riel in his trial. In Winnipeg, Riel would have been judged by a jury of 12, most likely a mix of French Métis and English settlers. In Regina, he faced six white, English-speaking Protestants. How this could be construed as a jury of his peers is hard to fathom. The territorial justice system affected Riel's trial in other ways as well. Frequent difficulties with translation cropped up, and key French-speaking witnesses often struggled to communicate in a language that was not their own.

The Act also allowed for the trial to be conducted by a magistrate instead of a judge. The difference was painfully significant. A judge was more experienced and enjoyed guaranteed job security. A magistrate, as defined by the legislation, was simply a lawyer who had at least five years' experience in the provinces. The government could then appoint him to try cases as a judge, but he enjoyed no security of tenure. A magistrate received a generous stipend upon which he, in all probability, had become dependent, but he could be appointed and dismissed at the pleasure of the government.

Thus magistrates were generally loyal party men, and such was certainly the case with Hugh Richardson, who was a true blue Tory. In addition to his position as a magistrate, he was also a paid legal advisor to Lieutenant-Governor Dewdney—in other words an insecure employee of the same government that, as far as Louis Riel was concerned, was also on trial.

Richardson had clearly been partisan before the trial, blaming the events of the North-West Rebellion on the bad influence of Louis Riel, who was also responsible for the Manitoba troubles of 1870. From the beginning, it was obvious that Richardson thought little of the organized democratic protest Riel had advocated; his bias continued to reveal itself throughout the trial. He allowed hearsay—secondhand information and testimony—evidence on behalf of the prosecution and, before retiring to deliberate on a verdict, charged the jury not to judge Riel's case on the evidence presented in the trial alone.

"You must think of society at large. You are not called upon to think of the government in Ottawa simply as a government; you have to think of the homes and of the people in the country, you have to ask yourselves: Can such a thing be permitted?"

The trial took place in a tiny brick courthouse built only a year before. A mere 50 by 20 feet, the assembled lawyers, witnesses, reporters and spectators were crammed in cheek by jowl. The first thing Riel's defense did was to challenge the jurisdiction of the court and the authority of Richardson. The objections were presented

The two-story brick building that housed Riel's trial had just been built. It could barely contain all the spectators for his court case.

thoroughly and with ample backing of precedent, but magistrate Richardson would have none of it. He dismissed the objections summarily in an economical, if completely unexplained and unjustified veto. The upshot was that this lowly territorial court, arguably imbued with the least legal standing in the country, was to try a charge of treason, "the highest crime known to the law," in a case that many considered to be the most important in Canadian history.

But perhaps that was the point.

"I guess the idea is to hang him," a smiling Alexander David Stewart, Hamilton police chief and Orangeman selected by the government to swear out the indictment on Riel, said to an Ontario journalist while being interviewed about the case.

The trial was short and sweet, as far as those who wanted to see Riel drop from the gallows were concerned. Many amongst Québec's elite rushed to Riel's aid, establishing the National Association for the Defense of the Imprisoned Métis. The association paid for Riel's legal fees and selected his lawyers, who were led by two able hotshots, Francois-Xavier Lemieux and Charles Fitzpatrick. Riel was overjoyed at the prospect of being represented by two such accomplished men and quickly sent a letter to his lawyers, summarizing the reasons behind the rebellion.

Lemieux replied in a similarly optimistic, if clipped, vein: "Your admirable letter has been received and creates great enthusiasm, great prospects."

It is true that Louis' correspondence left quite an impression on the lawyers. While still in Québec, Riel's future counsel was heard saying that if his client was guilty at all, he was culpable only of "the folly of loving his country too much." Yet when the French legal team met finally met their client on July 16, they quickly changed their opinion.

"We visited Riel today," the legal team wrote to Archbishop Taché, "and his words, his deportment and his conduct in general confirm that he was not of sound mind."

What exactly happened in the meeting is unknown, but it is not difficult to imagine Riel's hard-nosed counsel listening in growing disbelief and discomfort as, in the course of conversation, Riel excitedly expounded upon his belief that he was a prophet and that the North-West was divinely ordained to be divided amongst the nations of earth. They actually went easy on Riel when they informed Father Taché of his disturbed state of mind. When talking about their client amongst themselves, however, the lawyers tended to be severe in their judgment. Fitzpatrick believed Riel to be a "madman or a damned hypocrite, maybe both."

There is no reason to believe that their opinion of Louis' mental health was not genuine. After meeting him, they sincerely believed he was mad. It followed, therefore, that they planned to defend Riel on the grounds of insanity—to prove that he was incapable of distinguishing right from wrong during the rebellion, and therefore could not be held responsible for his actions. They decided that insanity was to be their only defense. Thus, the legitimacy of Louis' protests against the government were completely compromised, conducted, as the defense would maintain, by a madman.

This defense opened Louis up to all sorts of slander from his enemies. The most well-known example was the testimony from none other than Charles Nolin, Louis' estranged cousin. Nolin proved an almost unbelievably hostile witness. Louis knew that Nolin had deserted the Métis after the battle of Duck Lake, and he had always suspected that his cousin still harbored hidden resentments after their political standoff in Manitoba over 15 years previous. But he had no idea how deeply Nolin's ire ran until he was forced to listen to his cousin's virulent tirade against him.

Nolin was determined to get Louis once and for all, and even the Crown seemed embarrassed by the vindictiveness of his testimony. He stated, for example, that Riel had shown him a private book of his plans written in buffalo blood, and claimed that Riel had really only led the agitation to extort money from the government for his own selfish purposes.

This was too much for Riel, who interrupted and asked that he be allowed to speak in his own defense and cross-examine the hostile witness. His counsel responded immediately, cutting Louis' legs out from under him.

"For the last two days we felt ourselves in this position," Fitzpatrick addressed the court, "that our client is actually obstructing the proper management of his case, and he must be given to understand immediately that he won't be allowed to interfere with it, or

Louis Riel facing the court

else it will be absolutely useless for us to endeavor to continue any further in it."

Riel replied with eloquent generosity. "My counsel come from Québec, from a far province. They have to put questions to men with whom they are not acquainted, on circumstances which they don't know. They lose more than three-quarters of the good opportunities of making good answers from the witnesses. Not because they are not able; they are learned, they are talented, but the circumstances are such that they cannot put all the questions." He begged the court to be allowed to pose questions to Nolin himself.

Stodgy Richardson granted Riel no leeway, however, commanding the defendant to stop interrupting.

being lawyer

"Are you defended by counsel or not?" he asked a shaken Riel.

Louis would not abandon his counsel and so was forced to remain mute, although he believed his lawyers were missing opportunities for effective interrogation. What questions might he have raised, what line of defense might he have pursued had he defended himself? Given Louis' wide intellectual variation between political brilliance and disturbed religious musing, it is impossible to say.

As it was, he was caught between an accusation and a defense, neither of which he agreed with. The Crown was doing all it could to show that he was guilty of a charge that he had a rational and convincing argument against, while his own lawyers were trying their utmost to prove that he was insane, a position that he defied just as vehemently as the charge of treason against him.

Riel believed that he was perfectly sane, and had regular confrontations with his lawyers about his own state of mind. The idea that he might go down in history with the taint of insanity on his and his family's name was loathsome to him. Riel wanted to pursue a very different and far bolder tack in his defense, arguing that his conduct during the rebellion and his political career since 1869 were justified responses to a government that had blatantly disregarded the democratic right of his people. As intriguing as such a case might have been for the historical record, his lawyers refused to run with it, sticking to the insanity plea to the very end.

In any event, the debates on Louis' sanity, or lack of it, would only highlight a well-intentioned, though often sloppy case on the part of the defense. In sharp contrast, the prosecution was razor sharp. Led by some of the leading figures in Toronto's legal circles, the prosecution shot the insanity defense full of holes. Dr. Roy from Beauport, for example, agreed with the defense that Riel had relapsed into a "mental disease," which he termed "megalomania." Prosecutor Britton Bath Osler, however, so badgered the witness under cross-examination that Roy eventually admitted he was not an expert in insanity. So much for his testimony.

Despite such a score, however, this was the path upon which the Crown actually wanted Riel's defense to tread. For it gave the prosecutors a fairly easy case. After all, Riel had helped lead an armed rebellion against Canada: this was not at issue. To defend Riel on grounds of insanity effectively reversed the burden of proof, where the defense had to prove that Riel was insane, while dodging far thornier questions that might have been raised during the trial.

The defense's strategy skirted the principal issue of Louis' resistance against Ottawa—that the rebellion had actually been justified owing to government mismanagement and inaction. Indeed, when defense counsel moved in this direction while questioning Father André, the Crown quickly nudged them back onto the proper course.

"My learned friends have opened a case of treason, justified only by the insanity of the prisoner," the prosecution objected, "they are now seeking to justify armed rebellion for the redress of these grievances. These two defenses are inconsistent." So, headed off at the pass, the defense meekly returned to its singular track.

The greatest blows against the defense case came from Riel himself, however. He publicly congratulated the prosecution lawyers for shredding testimony suggesting he was insane. Further, in a dramatic speech just before the jury retired, Riel came across so reasonably, in such a dignified way, that it was simply impossible for the jurors to view the humble yet noble human before them as some sort of lunatic.

Nevertheless, as they retired to deliberate, it was clear that they harbored their doubts. For Riel had obviously regained some of the confidence that had been shattered after the rebellion was crushed, and in his speech to the jury he announced that he was a prophet to the New World while repeatedly making references to his divine mission in the North-West. Though the defense had failed to legally prove that Riel was insane, there was clearly some speculation among the jurors about Riel's mental health. In a letter to Liberal leader Edward Blake, another juror revealed that their doubts had taken another tack.

"We felt that had the government done their duty and redressed the grievances of the Half-breeds of Saskatchewan, there never would have been a second Riel Rebellion, and consequently no prisoner to try and condemn."

What might have happened if Riel's counsel had actively pursued a defense on these grounds?

In any case, these doubts came across in the verdict. The foreman trembled and tears flowed as he struggled to tell the courtroom that he and his fellows had reached the only verdict they could, given the trial that had just reached its conclusion. Riel was guilty of high treason. The clerk confirmed the sentence, at which point the foreman broke in, recommending that mercy be shown the prisoner.

None was forthcoming, nor could it have been in a case of high treason. And like a pagan priest intoning an age-old ritual of human sacrifice, Magistrate Richardson spoke the traditional sentence of corporal punishment.

"On the 18th of September next you will be taken to the place appointed for your execution and there be hanged by the neck until you are dead. May God have mercy on your soul."

The morning of November 16, 1885, in Regina was one of those beautiful dawns that herald the coming winter. The day was clear, the hoarfrost sparkled in the sunlight and the crimson-streaked prairie sky shone with the cold luminescence.

At 8 AM, a line of figures emerged from the jail. A priest led the way, followed by Riel and an escort of red-coated police. Father André brought up the rear. In tacit solemnity, they ascended the staircase to the gallows. When they reached the top, the procession stopped as Riel knelt to receive his final absolution from the two priests.

Riel had returned to the fold. In the time between the trial and the execution, Father André, who had acted as his confessor during his final days, had managed to persuade him to renounce those planks of his religious thought that were deemed heretical.

The last words Riel would ever write were: "I die Catholic and in the only true faith."

Louis may have considered himself lucky that he was granted the extra time for this final conversion. After Richardson sentenced him to death, a public furor erupted in the East. Fervent controversy and a flurry of appeals turned Riel's conviction into a political maelstrom. Outrage in Québec practically exploded upon the country. Riel came to be seen as a symbol of French Canada's fate at the hands of Anglo-Saxon Protestant Canada. The newspapers and public opinion were transfixed by the symbolic struggle to gain mercy for Riel. Thousands gathered at rallies to hear indignant nationalist politicians denounce the conviction. French-Canadian members of Macdonald's cabinet felt the heat.

On the other hand, Macdonald's government felt its collective hair curl from the vengeful bonfire that Ontario had become in the wake of the 1885 Rebellion. There could be no mercy as far as Orange Ontario was concerned. Macdonald's office suffered a deluge of telegrams and letters to that effect after the trial verdict. One of them threatened that if Riel was reprieved, "in a few months there will be the greatest rebellion, one of the mightiest struggles for freedom and liberty from French domination by the loyal, intelligent Protestant people of Ontario that our beloved Dominion has ever witnessed." Again the patriots-cum-bigots of Orange Ontario deemed themselves judge and jury as to what constituted a justifiable rebellion.

In the end, Macdonald sided with the English Canadians. In an infamous quote, the country's first prime minister dismissed the concerns of French Canadians with rank finality.

"Riel," he said, "shall hang though every dog in Québec bark in his favor."

Riel's case was appealed, but efforts had proven fruitless. Under pressure, Macdonald's Conservatives had established a commission to investigate Riel's sanity. Three doctors were appointed to give their opinion. It was a show engineered to justify Riel's sentence.

All of the men were picked by Macdonald and had good reason to exhibit their fidelity to his party.

One, however, refused his role in the charade. After his interviews, Dr. Francois-Xavier Valade concluded that, although he found Riel quite sane and capable in most respects, he found him unable to distinguish between what was right and what was wrong when it came to political and religious subjects. Dr. Valade's professional opinion was that such a failing surely indicated a form of insanity. Fortunately for Macdonald, his man on the spot, Lieutenant-Governor Dewdney, misrepresented Valade's report so egregiously that the Commons Committee believed that all three doctors had judged Riel sane. Ironically, Louis would have agreed with this finding. The execution was to proceed.

And so it was that Riel found himself on top of a scaffold in the chill early morning air, receiving his last rights. In his cell the night before, the last few hours of his life slipping away, his thoughts had returned to his faith and his family, and he composed one final, touchingly humble letter to his loved ones:

> Yesterday and today I have prayed God to strengthen you and grant you all his gentle comfort so that your heart may not be troubled by pain and anxiety.
>
> I embrace you all with the greatest affection.
>
> You, dear mother, I embrace you as a son whose soul is full of filial devotion.
>
> You, my dear wife, I embrace you as a Christian husband in the Catholic spirit of conjugal union.
>
> My dear little children, I embrace you as a Christian father, blessing you to the full extent of divine mercy both for the present and for the future.
>
> You my dear brothers and sisters, brothers- and sisters-in-law, nephews, cousins and friends, I embrace you all with all the cordiality of which my heart is capable.

Please be joyful,
Dear Mother,
I am your affectionate, submissive and obedient son
Louis David Riel

As Father André administered the last rites he asked Riel, "For the love of God do you forgive your enemies, all those who had desired and worked for your death?"

"I forgive them with all my heart as I would ask God to forgive me," Riel responded firmly. Such generosity of spirit was not to be reciprocated.

The hangman had been a prisoner at Fort Garry during the resistance, and as he slipped the noose over Riel's head he whispered the cold triumph of his vengeance in Louis' ear. A few more fragile seconds and the catch was released. The door swung open. The long fall. The sudden jerk and then the sway of the straining, weighted rope. It was over.

"The goddamn son of a bitch is gone at last," came a voice from the spectators.

"Yes," another chimed in, "the son of a bitch is gone at last."

List of Rights

Epilogue

LOUIS RIEL'S BODY was transported to Manitoba on December 10, 1885. Carried to his mother's home in St. Vital, Riel lay in state there for two days as Métis from all over the province came to pay their respects. Louis' mother, Julie, was inconsolable at the death of her dearest child, and she spent much of the time in the solitude of her bedroom. Marguerite Riel had contracted tuberculosis and was nearly incapacitated as she sat in a feverish delirium next to her husband's coffin.

On December 12, they buried Louis Riel. Hundreds of mourners gathered outside the Riel home to follow the pallbearers in procession for the six-mile funeral march to St. Boniface Cathedral. Rumors had been circulating that a group of Orangemen was planning to attack the procession, and every Métis man in the long column of mourners had a rifle slung over his back and one keen eye fixed on his surroundings. A political firebrand all his life, Louis was able to stir up trouble between Protestant and Catholic, Canadian and Métis even in death. But no attack came, and Riel was buried peacefully next to his father, just as he had requested.

The years after Louis' death were not kind to his clan. His wife succumbed to tuberculosis less than a year later, on May 24, 1886. Louis' daughter, Marie-Angélique, died of diphtheria in 1897, just before her 14th birthday. Louis and Marguerite's son, Jean, was a bright young man who eventually secured a job as a railway engineer. He married in 1908, but died that same year in a freak carriage accident just miles from St. Boniface. So it was that both of Louis Riel's direct descendents died young and childless. And so, Riel's immediate family, along with the traditional Métis way of life that he had given up his life to defend, did not live long after his own death.

Anyone living in the early 20th century who bothered to take stock of Louis Riel's life and accomplishments might easily conclude that he had failed utterly. Riel was an outlaw leader of a defeated rebellion, suspected by many to have been insane, yet still not crazy enough to be excused of high treason, executed, deprived of progeny and in possession of a dubious legacy. He hardly seemed to be the kind of man that history would judge as a success or, perhaps, even bother judging at all.

But then again, almost immediately after his execution, there were signs that Riel's stand against Ottawa had cast a deeper imprint on the Canadian psyche than anyone might have guessed. From the moment he was hanged, a major backlash against the Conservative government in Québec, which had largely acquiesced to Ottawa's policy during the North-West Rebellion, resulted in the ultimate downfall of the Tories in Québec.

The Anglo-Saxon subjugation of Louis Riel and the Métis rebellion in Saskatchewan defined the immediate future of western settlement, discouraged French Canada's ambitions past the 100th meridian and nudged Québec into an isolationist shell that would remain firm for the better part of a century. Yet given time, Riel's struggle against Orange Ontario's vision of Canada would gain cultural currency.

The bright sheen of the British Empire began to lose its luster in the 1900s, and Canadian historians undertook a reexamination of Louis Riel's place in the national mythology. Under the lens of post-Imperial inquiry, Riel's standing improved significantly. His heretofore well-documented psychological problems suddenly took a back seat to his democratic ideals. And where established historians had previously described him as a raving, rabble-rousing megalomaniac, more recent biographers began painting him as an able political advocate who had the courage to stand for his people against overwhelming odds. Recently, a popular movement has risen that aims to exonerate Riel from the charge of treason.

Thus, Louis Riel has taken his ambiguous place in national history. A homicidal traitor or a democratic visionary? A raving madman or a brilliant political mind undone by difficult circumstances? Just as Riel the man was immersed in controversy while he was alive, so too is Riel the historical figure marked by contention. Indeed, it's probably true that this controversy is precisely what keeps Louis' story alive in our own complex, highly contentious times. It is difficult for most of us today to relate to the monolithic national view of Orange Ontario, where it was imagined that a single Anglo-Saxon culture would sweep across the West and dominate the country. Instead, most contemporary Canadians' sympathies would naturally lean towards Louis Riel, who stood for an ideal much closer to the pluralistic society we currently inhabit.

Madman? Savior? Prophet? Politician? Many labels can be, and have been, attached to Louis Riel. Still, however the Métis leader is judged by us and subsequent generations, at the very least it can be said that he was a man possessed of a social imagination a few decades ahead of its time and a courage remarkable enough to see his vision turned to reality, no matter what the cost.

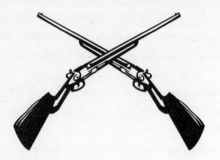

Notes on Sources

Allen, Robert K. and Frank Anderson. *The Riel Rebellion: 1885*.
Surrey: Frontier Books, 1984.

Beale, Bob and Rod Macleod. *Prairie Fire: The 1885 North-West
Rebellion*. Edmonton: Hurtig Publishers, 1984.

Bumsted, J.M. *Louis Riel v. Canada: The Making of a Rebel*.
Winnipeg: Great Plains Publications, 2002.

Coulter, John. *The Trial of Louis Riel*. Ottawa: Oberon Press,
1968.

Flanagan, Thomas, Ed. *The Diaries of Louis Riel*. Edmonton: Hurtig
Publishers, 1976.

Howard, Joseph Kinsey. *Strange Empire: The Story of Louis Riel*.
Ottawa: National Library of Canada, 1976.

McDougall, John. *In the Days of the Red River Rebellion*. Edmonton:
University of Alberta Press, 1983.

Siggins, Maggie. *Riel: A Life of Rebellion*. Toronto: HarperCollins,
1994.

Stanley, George Francis Gilman. *Louis Riel*. Toronto: McGraw Hill,
1963.

Woodcock, George. *Gabriel Dumont*. Montréal: Lidec, 1979.